In This Age of Confu... ...nflict, Prophetic Voices Urge Us to Wake Up

If you've ever felt like you don't have enough information about an issue, that you should wait to see what others do first, or that your voice won't make a difference, you're not alone.

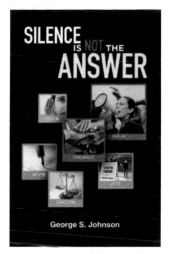

In *Silence Is Not the Answer*, George S. Johnson—author of *Courage to Think Differently* and *Beyond Guilt*—presents a collection of prophetic voices urging us to wake up, notice what is happening, and take a stand. The book offers viewpoints from a variety of writers—Walter Brueggemann, Bishop Herbert Chilstrom, Marcus Borg, Larry Rasmussen, Vivian Elaine Johnson, Jim Wallis, Sallie McFague, and others who encourage us to break the silence, not by shouting down others but by starting a real conversation.

"Johnson has assembled a cast of writing witnesses who . . . offer crisp, terse testimony to the urgency of gospel justice concerning a range of current issues."
—**Walter Brueggemann**, *Professor Emeritus, Columbia Theological Seminary*

"Johnson shows how silence becomes complicity and offers a variety of methods for both clergy and community advocates to raise their voices and be heard in today's moral wilderness."
—**Felicity Figueroa**, *community activist and Chair, Orange County Equality Coalition and Great American Write-In*

Praise for *Silence Is Not the Answer*

"All those who want their faith recentered on the radical call of Jesus should read this book."

> —Bishop Dr. Guy Erwin, Southwest California Synod, Evangelical Lutheran Church in America

"Reading the chapters of this book, I could not help but recall the telegram that Gerhart Riegner, secretary of the World Jewish Congress, sent on August 8, 1942, calling for the powers that be to acknowledge Hitler's plan to exterminate all the Jews of Europe. In the United States, his message was met with total silence. Thank you, George and Vivian, for sounding a warning and calling for our response."

> —Dr. Paul Wee, retired Senior Representative in Berlin, The Lutheran World Federation

"George's 'Letter to My Bishop' was so powerful. . . . When I finished the book, I was literally in tears. The book conveyed my theology, and I no longer felt so alone in the world. It convinced me that I cannot remain passive; our humanness, our identity, and our soul depend on action on our pressing contemporary issues."

> —Myrna Christopherson Kysar, retired pastor, Evangelical Lutheran Church in America

"George Johnson has pulled together another 'growing edge' book that calls us to consider more deeply the ways in which we break the silences."

> —Rev. James M. Lawson, Jr., teacher (1958–1968) for Martin King and John Lewis

"From George's and other authors' prophetic words, I find inspiration, energy, and hope at this critical time as I hear the cry of all creation. Vivian Johnson's 'Why I March' is wonderfully informative. I appreciate George's honesty in the preface as he breaks the silence personally and professionally. May this book spur a movement in the church."

—Jane Affonso, Chair, South Coast Interfaith Council Justice and Peace Action Team

"As we drift toward greater economic inequality and fascism worldwide, with repeated lies and misrepresentation by governments and economic powers, those who cherish the concepts of peace and justice must speak out in many ways. The church is faithful when laity speaks as well as professionals. This is eloquently stated in this book."

—E. B. Koschmann, MD

"As a person especially concerned about the climate change problem, I appreciated the article 'Living on this Planet So Others Can Live' by Sallie McFague."

—Dr. James A. Martin, George Washington University

"We need all the encouragement that is to be found in this book. Johnson's compilation of short, powerful essays is a gift and provocation to progressive pastors everywhere. We must straddle the chasm between an expressed congregational need for comfortable optimism and our prophetic urges to confront evil, injustice, and oppression in their many forms."

—Rev. Paige Eaves, Board President, Progressive Christians Uniting

"Once again, George Johnson has assembled an amazing group of wise and passionate voices who challenge us to 'do justice, love mercy, and walk humbly with our God.' The variety of topics and short essays makes this an excellent resource for not only individuals but for churches, study groups, and community organizations."

—Dave Ellingson, retired professor, pastor, and adventure kayaker

"Elie Wiesel famously wrote, 'What hurts the victim most is not the cruelty of the oppressor but the silence of the bystander.' Johnson has taken this admonishment to heart and created a volume of wisdom that will both guide and challenge us as we speak out against the many injustices we face during these difficult times."

—Rabbi Stephen J. Einstein, DHL, DD, HaRav Shalom Ya'akov ben Shaya, Zalman v'Zelda, Founding Rabbi Emeritus, Congregation B'nai Tzedek, Fountain Valley, California

"A clear and urgent call to action! George Johnson draws on the wisdom of diverse voices to add to his own prophetic voice. *Silence Is Not the Answer* inspires and empowers us all to explore, discern, and act on the urgent issues facing our world today. With contributions ranging from academia to down-to-earth personal experiences, every reader will be touched and moved to action by this book."

—Su Kraus, business owner

"There may be cases where silence is resistance like Jesus refusing to respond to the high priest's efforts to trap him—but too often silence is a lack of courage in the face of evil. The good news is that the voices in this book refuse to remain silent, knowing perhaps that 'the stones would cry out ' (Luke 19:40) otherwise."

—Joerg Rieger, Distinguished Professor of Theology, Vanderbilt University

"This book is for all who wish to foster enduring positive change in how we think, speak, act, and feel in matters of the self, others, and the wider world. George Johnson has once again discerned a key theme for our time."

—Philip Johnson, PhD, President, Finlandia University

"The list of contributors and their topics is all I need to add my voice to the chorus of gratitude for this publication."

—Dr. David L. Tiede, President Emeritus, Luther Seminary

"*Silence Is Not the Answer* is a much-needed collective challenge to all American Christians to find their voices and speak out against the divisive and hateful trends of our present day and proclaim a gospel of inclusion, love, justice, and respect for the dignity of all."

—Canon Brian J. Grieves, retired Peace and Justice Officer, Episcopal Church

"These are superb examinations of the interplay between divine grace and human love of neighbor, especially in arenas of peace and justice."

—Charles Lutz, longtime Lutheran advocate for Christian action on peace and justice concerns and advocate in Minnesota for just peace in the Holy Land

"Johnson has sent all of us an existential challenge from the twilight of his long and inspiring career. We are reminded that to be true followers of Jesus means to be willing to risk everything, even our own lives, to say loud and clear we will not be silent in the face of injustice."

—Howard B. Emery, MD

"This book, edited by my friend George Johnson, is an invaluable resource for those activists who want to be inspired, motivated, and nurtured by the experiences and wisdom of others who are in the same struggle for justice, sustainability, and wholeness. The matrix of seeking justice requires us all. Thank you, George."

—Mavis Anderson, Senior Associate, Latin America Working Group, Washington, DC

"Through the nineteen different authors, the Holy and disturbing Spirit pricked my conscious, touched my heart, aroused my values, and motivated me to add my voice to the chorus of caring and prophetic voices that so desperately need to be heard. In these pages, the passion of the Spirit, the priorities of the Kingdom, and the heart of God are calling us to wake up, speak up, get involved, and pay the price that is required to be faithful in our day."

—Howie Wennes, Bishop Emeritus, Grand Canyon Synod, Evangelical Lutheran Church in America

Silence Is Not the Answer

Do justice,
Love kindness,
Walk humbly.
(Micah 6:8)

George & Vivian Johnson

George S. Johnson

Summit Run Press

Summit Run Press
360 E. First Street, #451
Tustin, CA 92780
www.summitrunpress.com

Ordering Information

Quantity sales. Special discounts are available on quantity purchases by corporations, associations, and others. For details, contact the "Special Sales Department" at the address above.

Orders by US trade bookstores and wholesalers. Please contact BCH: (800)–431–1579 or visit www.bookch.com for details.

Printed in the United States of America

Cataloging-in-Publication Data

Names: Johnson, George S., 1933–, editor.
Title: Silence is not the answer / [edited by] George S. Johnson.
Description: Includes bibliographical references and index. | Tustin, CA: Summit Run Press, 2019.
Identifiers: LCCN 2019940093 | ISBN 978-0-9987689-5-3
Subjects: LCSH Social justice—Religious aspects—Christianity. | Church and social problems. | Christianity and justice. | Social change—Religious aspects—Christianity. | Religion and social problems. | Christians—Political activity. | Christian sociology. | Christian ethics. | BISAC RELIGION / Christian Living / Social Issues | RELIGION / Essays | SOCIAL SCIENCE / General | SOCIAL SCIENCE / Essays
Classification: LCC BR517 .S55 2019 | DDC 261.8092/273—dc23

First Edition

23 22 21 20 19   10 9 8 7 6 5 4 3 2 1

Special Thanks

About midway into the completion of this book I was diagnosed with Alzheimer's disease. My wife, Vivian; our daughters, Sonja and Joy; and I gave serious thought as to whether I should continue with the book. I knew It would be a lot of work for Vivian since my eyesight and hearing are limited.

Vivian gave me the green light, knowing how much the book meant to me. It was agreed that we should hire a professional editor and that Vivian would be my assistant editor and encourager. Those who have attempted to write a book know how much hard work is needed to seek permissions, edit copy, and prepare a manuscript for publication. I hereby dedicate this book with deep appreciation to my intelligent, compassionate, and gifted wife, *Vivian Elaine Johnson.*

Her skills, insights, and suggestions have made this book possible. Vivian has been my devoted wife and partner for fifty-nine years. She has been my critic, encourager, and caregiver. Together, we have survived many challenges. I hope many readers of this book will have the opportunity to thank Vivian for the role she played in its completion.

ALL IT TAKES IS one person to change the conversation. One person to take a risk, try something new, push against the status quo, and say this isn't right and here's what we can do about it.

You don't have to be a lawyer or a celebrity or a survivor to effect change. You just have to believe in something and fight for it. There are everyday trailblazers among us.

—ANITA HILL

Contents

Foreword

MANY OF US ARE alarmed and somewhat confused about what's happening in our country. This book gives us short, thought-provoking essays from God-grounded activists. They draw from biblical and other spiritual resources to inspire us to speak up and take action on social problems such as hunger and injustice, the resurgence of racism, neglect of climate change, and threats to our democracy.

George Johnson and the other leaders he features in this book focus on our tendency to keep quiet about controversial social issues. Several of the essays are about the pressure many preachers feel to not offend their congregations. Social pressure to not rock the boat sometimes keeps us from even thinking straight about some of the causes of suffering in our communities.

This book offers spiritual resources to think incisively—then speak up, march, organize, communicate with elected officials, and get involved in electoral campaigns. We can and should take *effective action* to make the world more consistent with the fact that God loves everybody.

George Johnson has been a leader on hunger and justice issues for decades. He is now suffering from Alzheimer's Disease, but that hasn't stopped him (together with his wife, Vivian) from completing this book. As George's mental capacities have declined, God's presence within him shines through even more clearly, and he has become even more bold in saying what he thinks needs to be said about harmful social systems.

As George writes, "Breaking the silence is our calling as the proclaimers of God's word and the agents of God's love."

David Beckmann
President, Bread for the World
April 2019

Preface

I HAVE ALZHEIMER'S DISEASE. Nothing to brag about, nothing to be ashamed about, and I see no reason to be silent about it. My brain served me well for eighty-five years, but now it has more and more difficulty remembering things. I decided not to spend the remaining days of my life dwelling on what I have lost. Instead, I want to give people resources that will help them think and act critically in an age of confusion and conflicting voices.

While I come from a Christian background, the points in this book pertain to people of all faiths, cultures, races, and genders. The main premises of *Silence Is Not the Answer* are for all people to read and act on.

I have read widely these past years about theology, politics, and suffering and its root causes. I cannot recall all that I have learned, but I can refer you to authors and spiritual leaders who I believe will challenge your preconceptions and give you hope for the future.

One of my favorite authors and theologians at this stage in my life is Marcus J. Borg. His book *Jesus: Uncovering the Life, Teachings, and Relevance of a Religious Revolutionary* is a masterful portrayal of the historical Jesus and emerging Christianity. He explores the way Jesus resisted the domination system of the Roman empire power of his day. For Borg, both the personal and the political dimensions of Jesus's message are important for understanding the revolutionary aspects of his life and teaching. I highly recommend Borg's book if you want to understand who Jesus is for Christians today.

Another theologian I find inspiring is Leonardo Boff, a Roman Catholic priest from Brazil whose speaking out about the suffering of the poor and the death of millions in Latin America made headline news. Despite attempts by the church to silence Boff because his speech was offensive to the establishment, his message made a difference. Boff's book *When Theology Listens to the Poor* is a call for the modern church to create a better option for the poor. He points out how Matthew 26:11, "The poor you will always have with you," is used to support the status quo and creates an attitude of fatalism, pessimism, and cynicism that destroys any hope that things could be different. However, Boff argues that the true meaning of this verse is that the opportunity to help is always there. Boff reminds us that when Jesus offered a better option for the poor, he was making it clear that God acts to free people from the bondage of poverty and oppression. It is the prophetic task of the church to do the same.

Some people may say, "I don't remember George espousing such progressive positions in his previous writings. Has he changed his mind?" In the past, I sometimes felt that I didn't have enough information about an issue, that others had good points too, that I should wait to see what happened, and that my voice wouldn't make a difference. But these excuses allowed bad choices to be made that cause suffering for our brothers and sisters. As Brian McLaren says in his book *The Great Spiritual Migration*, we are all in the process of development. Sometimes new wine needs new wineskins, as Larry Rasmussen says.

I have a certain perspective. My education and life experience have shaped my thinking and analyses. Others will see things differently. I respect that. But as Holocaust survivor Elie Wiesel says, "What hurts the victim most is not the cruelty of the oppressor but the silence of the bystander."[1] We need to read and listen attentively and then speak out for causes that we think are important. John the Baptist is described in the Gospels as "the voice of one crying out in the wilderness."[2] He calls us to "repent,"[3] wake up, and change. *Silence Is Not the Answer* is a collection of prophetic voices urging us to wake up, notice what is happening, and take a stand. Our world today is filled with fear, conflict, war, and confusion. I encourage you to read the writers in this book with an open mind and think about their urgent cry.

Some points will be made more than once. Some truths are worth repeating. When I say to my wife, "I love you," I'm glad that Vivian doesn't say, "George, you already told me that."

When I began putting this book together, my wife said, "With your diminished hearing and eyesight and your memory problems, are you able to tackle another book?" Maybe not, but some things need to be said as we move toward the 2020 elections and beyond. So, with the help of Vivian and a professional editor, I collected some pieces written by myself and others to let our voices be heard and break the silence.

If we remain silent, then our leaders and fellow citizens will not wake up and change course. We must speak up and take action now before our society is beyond saving.

Part I

Breaking the Silence

WHAT DO WE MEAN by breaking the silence? Whose task is it? In what way is it a theological task? Which silences need to be broken and why? How do we go about it?

Breaking the silence is deciding that remaining silent is not helpful or necessary. Thomas Johnson reminds us that when the German church remained silent during the Third Reich's rise to power, it enabled Hitler to use nationalism to support his hatred of Jews. Dietrich Bonhoeffer's willingness to speak out was a wake-up call to the church in Germany to pay attention to what was happening. For the most part, the church remained silent, and the rest is history.

Wesley Granberg-Michaelson also urges us to pay attention to rhetoric and policies that conflict with our moral values. In such cases, our faith calls us to speak out against the secular authorities that push agendas of hatred and greed.

Breaking the silence means joining others in taking a stand on important issues. A sense of community develops among those who share your values. A power is released when people join others in speaking out. Vivian Johnson shares the many reasons why she marches and reminds us that those in power rarely initiate progress—change starts with people on the ground.

There are many different ways to break the silence. Old Testament scholar Walter Brueggemann suggests that prayer is also a form of silence breaking. It is a way to expose the suffering and hurts of people and of creation. In the introduction to his book *Interrupting Silence: God's Command to Speak Out*, he uses biblical passages and pivotal points in the history of social justice to illustrate the importance and the power of breaking the silence. According to Brueggemann, even the church has been guilty of being a silencer. He claims that the urgent prophetic task of the church today is to break the silence on important issues.

Jim Wallis, editor and founder of *Sojourners* magazine, points out the importance of discerning between the ideology of the state and that of the Bible. He draws parallels between the Nazi regime and the Trump presidency to demonstrate that when the church gives uncritical support to a corrupt leader, it becomes an arm of the state rather than a much-needed voice of truth.

Theologian John Cobb notes that a lack of thoughtful criticism can be found on both sides of the political aisle. Many liberals who speak out against Trump's policies today remained silent when past Democratic administrations enacted similar policies. Cobb urges us to set aside petty partisanship and speak up for causes such as peace, justice, and sustainability.

Christine Smith, author of *Preaching as Weeping, Confession, and Resistance: Radical Responses to Radical Evil*, demonstrates that preaching is an act of resistance as well as a declaration of good news. She argues that breaking the silence is essential to ending societal evils such as male chauvinism and violence against women. People and institutions of faith are in a unique position to demand justice for victims of violence and healing for communities infested with it.

Richard Rohr, a Roman Catholic priest, observes that we are used to thinking and acting within set boundaries imposed by society—and questioning those boundaries is discouraged. But because we are also citizens of the kingdom of God, we are emancipated and freed to think outside the box and speak up about alternative ways to achieve justice and equality.

As these writers demonstrate, breaking the silence that surrounds important issues like social justice and peace can be done in many ways—by praying, by marching, by preaching, or simply by speaking up. However you choose to do it, breaking the silence is our calling as the proclaimers of God's word and the agents of God's love.

Is This a Bonhoeffer Moment?

⇒ Thomas K. Johnson ⇐

DIETRICH BONHOEFFER WAS ONE of the first victims of Nazi censorship. On February 1, 1933, just a couple of days after Adolf Hitler was appointed chancellor of the Weimar Republic, Bonhoeffer chose to speak out and share his concerns about this new leader.

Bonhoeffer went on the radio to warn that "if a leader surrenders to the wishes of his followers, 'then the image of the Leader (*Führer*) will gradually become the image of the misleader (*Verführer*).'"[1] He was mysteriously cut off before he finished his speech. This was the first attempt to silence Bonhoeffer, but as his works and his life demonstrated, remaining quiet and compliant wasn't the answer for him. He eventually sacrificed his life by speaking out, and he inspired others to protest injustice and hate, even to this day.

Some see our current political climate as a Bonhoeffer moment. Notable Bonhoeffer scholars Stephen Haynes, Michael DeJonge, Lori Brandt Hale, and Reggie Williams offer a critical analysis of Bonhoeffer's relevance to our current situation. They note various similarities between Hitler's regime and Trump's presidency, such as the rise of nationalism, attacks on the free press, a powerful propaganda machine that reinforces the same message over and over, blaming specific minorities for all the ills of society, and last but not least, a charismatic leader who uses people's fear and anger to reinforce blind loyalty. Other commonalities include attacks on the judicial system, attempts to remove all checks and balances, and suggestions of various conspiracies trying to undermine the powers that be. In light of these similarities, we are challenged to resist and speak out.

The problem is that this is also a Bonhoeffer moment for many evangelicals, though for very different reasons. Evangelicals see this as a time to finally take back America and make it a Christian country again. Now is their chance to challenge previous Supreme Court decisions upholding the legality of same-sex marriages and abortion. For evangelicals such as best-selling author Eric Metaxas, Bonhoeffer's emphasis on obedience to God's word and stringent discipleship means we should be advocates for conservative and biblical values.

So which interpretation of Bonhoeffer is the authentic one? Stephen Haynes, in *The Battle for Bonhoeffer*, attempts to answer this question by arguing that both sides should acknowledge the emphasis Bonhoeffer places on the Sermon on the Mount. According to Haynes, Bonhoeffer believed that "the Church is only the Church when it exists for others"[2] and the church's true mission is to serve the suffering. How, then, can any Christian defend separating children from their parents; discriminating based on race, religion, or economic status; dismantling health-care; or threatening to deport contributing members of society?

Are these not the kinds of questions Bonhoeffer would ask if he were alive today? Wouldn't he urge us to act responsibly and protest policies that promote injustice and dehumanize God's children?

Bonhoeffer believed that Christians had not only the right but the responsibility to ask whether their government is upholding justice and order and to aid any victims of the state. In Bonhoeffer's view, the church was obligated "not just to bind up the wounds of the victims beneath the wheel but to seize the wheel itself. Such an action would be direct political action on the part of the church."[3]

Bonhoeffer concluded that Christ aligned himself with those who are marginalized and suffering under the cruel actions of immoral leaders and corrupt governments. To Bonhoeffer, Christ would be present in the refugees seeking a safe haven and the immigrants hoping to find asylum from death squads. Christ would be present in those who speak the truth, not in those who spread lies and obstruct justice.

Isn't the authentic Bonhoeffer the one who boldly proclaims that Christ is present in all who suffer injustice rather than the one who is used to justify increased discrimination and the undermining of civil liberties?

Which Bonhoeffer would Trump embrace—and which would he try to silence? This is the question we need to ask if we want to know whether we are facing a time like Bonhoeffer's.

Bonhoeffer seems to give us his answer in an essay written to support the resistance ten years after Hitler took power: "Who stands firm? Only the one whose ultimate standard is not his reason, his principles, conscience, freedom, or virtue; only the one who is prepared to sacrifice all of these when, in faith and in relationship to God alone, he is called to obedient and responsible action. Such a person is the responsible one, whose life is to be nothing but a response to God's question and call."[4]

Bonhoeffer's own words illustrate the contrast between him and people who, like Trump, thirst after power and wealth, especially at the expense of others:

Judgment and action will distinguish those who follow Jesus in renouncing property, fortune, right, righteousness, honor, and power from the world. They become an offense to the world. For this reason, the disciples are persecuted for righteousness' sake. Not recognition but rejection is the world's reward for their word and work. It is important that Jesus also blesses his disciples when they suffer not directly for the sake of the confession of his name, but for the sake of a just cause. They are given the same promises as the poor. As the persecuted, they are indeed like the poor.[5]

Isn't this our challenge and calling? If we follow and obey Christ, then *every moment* is a Bonhoeffer moment. Whenever suffering and injustice occurs, are we not given the opportunity and the obligation to speak out, stand up, and take action for the welfare of all God's children?

Introduction to Interrupting Silence: God's Command to Speak Out

➡ Walter Brueggemann ⬅

SILENCE IS A COMPLEX matter. It can refer to awe before unutterable holiness, but it can also refer to coercion where some voices are silenced in the interest of control by the dominant voices. It is that latter silence that is the primary focus of the studies that follow.

On April 15, 1967, at Riverside Church in New York City, Martin Luther King, Jr., gave an address to Clergy and Laymen Concerned about Vietnam titled "Beyond Vietnam: A Time to Break the Silence." In that address, King not only spoke vigorously against the U.S. war policy in Vietnam, but he also linked opposition to the war to the crisis of race that he had long addressed. I remember that address; like many others at the time, I feared that in linking the war to the racial crisis King was detracting focus and energy away from the race crisis. But, of course, I, along with many others, was wrong. King understood that the war and race belonged to a cluster of issues, all of which flow together in a collusive silence in which public opinion had silently accepted top-down authority. King's breaking of the silence was a freighted moment in mobilizing sustainable opposition to the war in a challenge to settled authority.

King's capacity to break the silence that supported the war is representative of many movements that break the silence of long-protected practices of domination and exploitation. Most recently a number of church bodies have begun, albeit belatedly, to speak out against the church's pernicious, still-in-effect "Doctrine of Discovery" that long ago (and until now) cedes "the new world" to the old European colonizing powers, a ceding that currently feeds white nationalist sentiment in the United States. Such belated protests that work toward abrogation of that long-standing "doctrine" have come with an awareness that we must not be silent. In fact, many groups are now insisting that we must not be silent any longer, such as many liberation movements, among them feminism and womanism in many varieties, queer theology, Black Lives Matter, and voices of and for the disabled. In the Bible, perhaps the most vigorous character in such silence breaking is the importunate (nagging!) widow in Jesus' parable in Luke 18:1–8. All of these silence breakers have come to see that silence is a strategy for the maintenance of the status quo, with its unbearable distribution of power and wealth. Silence breakers characteristically insist that the old patterns of power must be disrupted and reconfigured. Thus the widow asked for and insisted on justice.

The silencers variously intend to maintain the status quo. In the ancient text the paradigmatic silencer is above all Pharaoh, a metaphor for all silencers, a company that comes to include, in the biblical tradition, kings, priests, scribes, and "the crowd" that was uncritically allied with such powers. We know very well in our time, moreover, that many voices are required for the maintenance of a democracy, and so the silencers resort to voter repression and gerrymandering—strategies for silencing those who would disrupt present power arrangements.

Thus, the ongoing historical process can be seen as an unequal contest between the silencers and those who would break the silence in the interest of new historical possibility. The contest is unequal because the silencers have better means of communication and control, not least management and ownership of most of the public media. In the world of the ancient text, "public media" meant especially the stylized practices of monarchy and temple. "Breaking the silence" is always counter-discourse that tends to arise from the margins of society, a counter to present power arrangements and to dominant modes of social imagination.

To be sure, the breaking of silence is not always positive and constructive, as some silence breakers may also yield destructive voices; we should not romanticize. A case in point of such negative silence breaking is that of the far-right political leader in the Netherlands, Geert Wilders, who lost an election for prime minister in March 2017. At the instant of his electoral defeat, he declared, "Regardless of the verdict, no one will be able to silence me." Another example is flag burning in the United States. It is such unwelcome speech, but it is protected by the Constitution. Nevertheless, President Trump wants to silence such activists by jail or revocation of citizenship. That, of course, is the risk of allowing for silence breaking, but it is a risk that is indispensable for any human society that is not to drift further toward fascism and the domination of a single voice.

The church has a huge stake in breaking the silence, because the God of the Bible characteristically appears at the margins of established power arrangements, whether theological or socioeconomic and political. The church at its most faithful is allied with artistic expression from the margin that voices alternatives to dominant imagination. Prayer—beyond conventional polite prayer—is an act of breaking the silence. Thus, in the parable of Luke 18:1–8,

Jesus tells the disciples to pray like the widow in the narrative: that is, "to pray always and not to lose heart" (v. 1). Intercession, that is, *intrusion into the courts of power on behalf of another*, is central to the church's action in prayer. Gerald Sheppard has, moreover, proposed that the lament and protest prayers of the book of Psalms that critique and assault enemies are designed for being "overheard" by those enemies, who are thereby called to account.

> We may argue that prayer even when spoken in private is a political activity. Prayer requires an economic use of times and places. Prayer seeks to articulate reality, attribute aspects of reality to God, summon God to act, and nurture courage to persevere or provoke change in the conduct of the one who prays. The question is, strictly speaking, not whether prayer is political, but what politics pertain to this or that particular prayer.

The studies offered here are discrete discussions of specific texts. The effect for me however, has been cumulative, and I hope it will be so for the reader. As I have moved from text to text, the company of silence breakers has become more evident to me. Since we now live in a society—and a world—that is fitfully drifting toward fascism, the breaking of silence is altogether urgent. In the institutional life of the church, moreover, the breaking of silence by the testimony of the gospel often means breaking the silence among those who have a determined stake in maintaining the status quo.

It is my hope that these sketches of silence will help us to discern more clearly the way in which our socio-political circumstance, now as always, is an urgent contest between silence and silence breaking. I hope as well that these sketches of silence may constitute a summons to sign on more vigorously with the silence breakers who know, deeply and intimately, that silence kills.

I finish with one more vignette concerning silencing from Lewis Hyde, who reports on a sermon by Charles Chauncy in 1742 titled "A Caveat against Enthusiasm." Chauncy fears the enthusiasts in his context who wanted to sing and dance in worship:

> Chauncy gives his flock instruction on how to recognize the enthusiasts in their midst. That you can't reason with them is the first sign, but, interestingly enough, all the others have to do with their bodies: "it may be seen in their countenance," "a certain wildness . . . in their general look," "it strangely loosens their tongues," "throws them . . . into quakings and tremblings," they are "really beside themselves, acting . . . by the blind impetus of a wild fancy." It is precisely the feeling that one's body has been entered by some "other" that Chauncy wishes to warn against.

Chauncy saw that such people preferred bodily action rather than talk:

> And the ceremonies of enthusiastic religions tend to include the body, rather than talk. The celebrants dance and sing, they quake and tremble. But no one dances ecstatic dances in the churches of the rich. Nor do they speak in tongues or raise their hands in the gesture of epiphany the way the Christian enthusiasts do. The rich would seem to sense that the more you feel the spirit move in the physical body on Sunday, the harder it will be to trade in cash on Monday. Better to sit in one's pew and listen to talk.

But Chauncy did not even mean "talk." More precisely he meant "listen to a talk," that is, to sit and listen in silence to an authorized voice. Hyde goes on to say that such talk in the church, dominated by "abstraction of symbols" in theology, is deeply linked to the abstract symbol of "cash," thus linking *abstract theology that silences* to the *reduction of life to commoditization and the management of money.* It is, Hyde judges in an appeal to Walt Whitman, reference to the body in its concreteness, which counters such abstractions, that permits domination, monopoly, and exploitation. It has struck me through these several textual studies how silence breaking is evoked by attention to the body in pain. The body knows that silence kills. When the silence is broken, the body may be restored and the body politic may be open to new possibility.

The Heresy of Ideological Religion

⇒ Jim Wallis ⇐

DIETRICH BONHOEFFER WAS A young pastor and theologian in Germany during the rise of Adolf Hitler. Bonhoeffer founded an underground seminary, where he helped to lead what became known as the Confessing Church. His fundamental question was always, "Who is Jesus Christ for us today?"

There are never exact analogues in history. But there are questions and challenges from 1930s Germany that we should learn from today.

The Confessing Church and the Barmen Declaration, its statement of theological resistance to Nazism written mostly by theologian Karl Barth, were not simply expressing political opposition to Hitler and Nazism. Their objections were theological, and Hitler's name was not even mentioned in the declaration. The issue for them was discipleship to Christ, as opposed to the uncritical support that many church leaders were offering to Hitler, creating in effect a "state church."

In the original German, Bonhoeffer's classic work *The Cost of Discipleship* was simply called *Disciple*. That was the issue for Bonhoeffer, Barth, and the courageous members of the Confessing Church: how they needed to *disciple* their church members against the ideological religion that the German churches were being infected with by the political regime.

Perhaps the most blatant recent example of a "state church" mentality in relation to Donald Trump was a tweet by Franklin Graham. "Never in my lifetime," the son of Billy Graham tweeted, "have we had a @POTUS willing to take such a strong outspoken stand for the Christian faith like @realDonaldTrump. We need to get behind him with our prayers." Such an uncritical, unprophetic, and ungodly devotion to such a deeply ethically compromised president does call to mind the complicit church in 1930s Germany.

Fox News is an important actor in the creation of a "state church" in this country. Pastors of more conservative churches often tell me, "It isn't even fair—I have them for an hour each week on Sunday; Fox News has them the whole rest of the week." Pastors can't compete with the 24/7 ideology preached by Fox.

The Barmen Declaration was clear about the separation that must be maintained between the church and the state. "We reject the false doctrine," the declaration said, that "the church . . . should and could appropriate the characteristics, the tasks, and the dignity of the state, thus itself becoming an organ of the state."

The presidency of Donald Trump has raised the question of whether this is a "Bonhoeffer moment." This goes far beyond partisan politics—many conservatives and Republicans, along with liberals and Democrats, are raising questions about the moral and religious issues at stake in the presidency of Donald Trump. Here are some of them.

First, let's start with truth, a central Christian concern. Many presidents lied when it served their political interests. In the Trump administration, lying has become persistent and pathological, occurring almost every day from the White House and the daily press briefing. No administration is ever happy with its press coverage, but the Trump administration's regular attack on the media as "fake news" is a dangerous assault on freedom of the press and the First Amendment.

Second, there is racial bigotry, another central Christian concern. From Trump's "birtherism" that questioned the identity of the first black president to his attacks on Mexican immigrants, from his Muslim bans to his appeals to the white nationalist base, Trump has used racial fear and hate to his political advantage. The racial divide in the church is creating what I call a "Corinthians crisis," where one part of the body of Christ—Christians of color—is suffering while the white part of the body of Christ is not feeling their pain. And how we treat the stranger—immigrants and refugees, all the "others" who are put before us—is for us a matter of theological obedience, not political partisanship.

Third, Trump's strongman style of leadership is a direct contradiction of the Christian ethic of servant leadership, and the civic ethic of public service, and points to the critical need for humility as well as checks and balances to restrain our political leaders.

Fourth, "America First" is a theological heresy. The body of Christ is the most racially and culturally diverse community on Earth—our connection to brothers and sisters all over the world makes our political convictions global, and not just national. And stewardship of the Earth, its resources and its people, is a priority for people of faith over an administration that shows no concern for God's creation.

Regardless of whether special counsel Robert Mueller indicts Trump, whether Trump fires the special counsel to try to forestall the investigation, or whether Congress impeaches him, theological integrity more than political partisanship must govern the churches' response.

Preaching: Breaking Silence

⇒ Christine M. Smith ⇐

NEW THEOLOGICAL NAMING INVOLVES the work of critique and deconstruction, but it also creates and bodies forth new understandings of religious meaning. As a result of women's naming, I have come to understand *breaking silence* as an essential theological concept in a theological agenda that would resist male domination. Breaking the silence of the violence that engulfs women's lives is a redemptive act that declares that the lives of girl children and adult women are holy and sacred and that violence is a distortion of our human relations. I want to turn now to a fuller exploration of breaking silence as the primary theological concept that might inform preaching ministries struggling against sexism and male domination.

There are three dimensions to this act of breaking silence that place it in the realm of saving, transforming activity. Breaking silence stops the cycle of violence, demands individual and community accountability, and begins the process of restoration and healing.

STOPPING THE CYCLE OF VIOLENCE

The cycle of violence must stop if there is ever to be movement toward justice and wholeness. When people break out of this silence, it is not just that they are responding to the individual, private lives of victimized women; they are also calling the entire structure of male supremacy into question. To break the silence about male violence is to stop the concrete behaviors that reinforce and maintain male domination. The church knows that this is true at a conscious and unconscious level, and thus it too often backs away in silence. This silence can be broken in many ways.

When a woman decides to leave her home and seek the safety of a woman's shelter, the silence of her oppression is broken. In that same act the silence and denial of male violence are shattered if only for a moment. This impulse to reach out for help is a movement toward life. When a girl child decides to tell a family friend that her father is sexually abusing her, the silence of her abuse is broken. In that same act the silence and denial of destructive family privacy and distorted male sexuality are shattered if only for a moment. This impulse to tell is a movement toward life. When a woman decides to press charges against an acquaintance who has raped her, the silence of her domination is broken. In that same act, the silence and denial of male ownership and supremacy are shattered if only for a moment. This impulse to hold accountable is a movement toward life.

These impulses toward healing, accountability, and transformation are movements toward a healthy sense of self, relationality, and community. The impulses come from a desire for survival itself and an end to violent abuse. They are faithful, saving acts. "Therefore, Christianity is not only a life of proclamation of the saving act of God in the past, but also a life of participation in and with the sanctifying grace of God in the present."[1] For women and men to break the silence and denial surrounding violence against women is to participate in the work of sanctification.

Marie Fortune believes that breaking the cycle of violence involves truth telling, deprivatization, deminimization, and protection for the vulnerable. Cycles of violence are broken as helping professionals acknowledge the breadth and depth of the violations that have occurred, expose the violence to public scrutiny, listen to and believe the stories of victims, and become advocates for protection for those who are at risk.[2]

Religious communities and preachers have much to learn from women and men working in direct human services with women who are victimized by violence. They understand with absolute clarity that the first step in responding to violence is to stop it. Women working with battered women's shelters respond *first* to the safety of the woman who is in danger. Psychologists and social workers respond *first* to the safety of children who are sexually abused. Women advocates who work directly with women who have been raped respond *first* to the immediate safety and needs of the woman who has been raped.

What makes this redemptive work so shocking for some is that it places girls and women in positions of ultimate importance and priority. The safety and lives of women are more important than the sanctity of marriage and the prerogatives of male sexuality. The safety and lives of girl children are more important than parental power and the privacy of the family. These are radical shifts in power and priority. The church should be deeply disturbed that most of the concrete services in this country that respond directly to violence against women have been created by women's advocacy groups outside the church. Pastors and preachers need to be confronted with the fact that these groups are literally saving people's lives because they are responding to the violence in women's lives in ways the church is not.

The literature suggests that when preachers are bold and clear in their sermons about issues related to woman battering, rape, or incest, women do come forward to speak with them in an attempt to break the silence and the violence. Even with full awareness of this truth, countless preachers remain painfully silent and participate in the church's larger denial. Or worse yet, preachers and pastors urge women to return to the cycle of violence. Not only blatant insensitivity keeps many preachers silent, but also much of our traditional theology encourages denial in a very insidious way.

Some of our traditional understandings of sin have provided a firm foundation on which silence and denial have thrived. In an article entitled "Evil, Sin, and Violation of the Vulnerable," Mary Potter Engel begins to construct a new understanding of sin from the perspective of a theology of liberation from sexual and domestic abuse. She explores four dimensions of a new understanding of sin that contribute to a liberating theology in response to violence against women, three of which are particularly relevant to breaking the silence surrounding violence. She renames sin as *distortion of feeling*, as *betrayal of trust*, and *as lack of care*.[3]

Christian theology has suggested that it is sinful to be angry and resistant. Human beings are to be self-sacrificing, slow to anger, and always loving. This definition of sin and its implications for righteous human behavior leave victimized women blaming themselves for the violence inflicted upon them. Women believe that if they had been more self-giving, less angry, and more loving, violence would not have occurred. Our traditional understandings of sin have robbed women and men of the power and impact of righteous indignation and healthy anger. Our Christian theology has traditionally stressed passive acceptance of the conditions of one's life. Anger and resistance are the epitome of sin.

In defining sin as a distortion of feeling, Engel makes two important theological moves. She shifts responsibility to perpetrators who distort and shatter right relation, while simultaneously encouraging women to express anger, indignation, and resistance in their own lives in ways that help terminate the violence. Engel also begins to develop an understanding of sin that is corporate in nature. The moral indifference of preachers and religious communities is named as the sin of distorted feelings. This understanding of sin compels preachers and religious communities to break into the cycle of violence and demands that we respond with outrage and resistance. "If all of us were to speak and act out against sexual and domestic abuse with the righteous indignation of the prophets, we would no longer be colluding in an oppressive system of violence."[4]

Christian theology has also suggested that sin has to do with the prideful arrogance of disobedience and self-love. These understandings have kept women and children silenced in their own victimization, and have kept preachers and religious communities believing that this suffering is necessary and righteous. Women are particularly vulnerable to an understanding of sin that suggests that all human beings have "crosses to bear." For many women and girl children violence and abuse become those totally justified crosses. "The central image of Christ on the cross as the savior of the world communicates the message that suffering is redemptive. If the best person who ever lived gave his life for others, then, to be of value we should likewise sacrifice ourselves."[5]

Women have been encouraged to love others at total expense to self, and dimensions of Christian theology have provided the moral and ethical underpinnings for such total self-sacrifice. Here again, Engel makes two very helpful theological moves. She suggests that sin is the act of betraying trust, not the act of disobedience. She also shifts the definition of sin from self-love to a lack of care. As an attempt to empower women who are victimized by violence she encourages women not to participate in the sinfulness of allowing the boundaries of their own self to be disregarded and violated. "Rather than speak of sin as pride or self-love to victims, we should speak of it as distortion of the self's boundaries."[6] Through both suggestions Engel helps us to understand that the sin of perpetrators is the betrayal of a trusted relationship, and the sin of women caught in the web of violence is a willingness to participate in their own victimization.

These understandings empower women and men to break out of the web of violence. They also shift our understanding of sin away from self-loathing and self-denial and direct us toward encouraging women to develop a sense of self-love and a genuine sense of power that will make them less vulnerable to the domination and abuse of male violence. Engel's new theological naming enables us to transform our understandings of sin in such a way that many levels of silence can be broken. Then distorted apathy and silence of society toward violence within trusted, known relationships can be broken, as well as the apathy and silence toward violence perpetrated by strangers.

Preachers have an opportunity to break the silence surrounding violence at many different levels. When we speak directly about woman battering, domestic violence, incest, and rape in our proclamations, we break the silence of denial. Our theological work breaks silence also as we rework aspects of traditional understandings of sin that perpetuate violence and proclaim liberating definitions that mobilize the Christian community's resistance. With new understandings of sin, preachers might be more fully empowered to break the silence of popular moral indifference, the silence of justification and betrayal in the lives of perpetrators, and the silence of women's conditioned complicity and powerlessness.

INDIVIDUAL AND COMMUNITY ACCOUNTABILITY

One of the profound repercussions of silence and denial is the privatization of the violence. As long as the church continues to believe that violence happens to isolated individuals in the privacy of homes, bedrooms, and darkened streets, individuals and whole communities are never held accountable. Pastors and preachers participate in this privatization. "Out of arrogance, embarrassment, ignorance, or feelings of helplessness, pastors often give the impression that violent control of women and children is sometimes a necessary part of family life and must be accepted."[7] Far too often, instead of preachers empowering individuals and communities to become increasingly responsive and accountable about violence, they accept the status quo with a haunting indifference. How might preachers move individuals and communities toward greater accountability?

It is not just the church's traditional theology about sin and suffering that has contributed to male domination and female oppression. There are deep, permeating strands of Christian theology that define females as fundamentally inferior human beings. The church's theology has often reduced women to objects as surely as has the larger society. Carole Bohn describes and critiques this web of dehumanizing theological assumptions about the superiority of males and the inferiority of females as a theology of ownership.[8] In examining the account of creation in Genesis 2 and 3 she describes the theology that flows from it in this way:

Man's authority to rule over woman is traced to God's intention in this account from Genesis 2 and 3. . . . Throughout history, laws of various societies have attempted to limit the extent and means of man's control, but the underlying message, built into the words and structures of religious tradition, remains constant. By God's design, women and children are subject to men.[9]

By its very nature, a theology of ownership keeps violence not only privatized and hidden, but also theologically condoned. If men *own* women and children, and are their moral, emotional, and physical superiors, this not only serves as a rationale for silence, but becomes a justification for men to indeed *control* that which they own. This theology of ownership contributes in a significant way to the silence and denial of churches and preachers.

Part of the power and distortion of patriarchy and male domination comes from their ability to structure lies into human consciousness and social structures. No human being owns another human being. No theological concept or belief justifies violent domination. Preachers must be very attentive and sophisticated in our critique of every aspect of Christian theology that suggests male domination is the natural order of creation. Dismantling this theology of ownership is in many ways an essential move toward individual and community accountability. It is not enough to simply respond to the violence itself; we also need to critique the underlying theology that helps to perpetuate it. Bohn critiques mainline denominations' pronouncements against violence that are devoid of deconstructive and constructive theologizing about the root causes. "While they call their churches to some sort of action, they do not challenge their institutions' historic stance toward and complicity with the problem. They are pragmatic attempts to confront the problem of domestic violence; yet they are primarily band-aids designed to alleviate a symptom."[10]

She goes on to suggest three concrete steps that must be taken to dismantle a theology of ownership. First, religious communities must begin to make connections between the personal and the political. There must be a shift from seeing acts of violence and the need for healing as individual matters to seeing violence and healing as communal and systemic matters. "It means that pastors, along with all other caregivers, will have to move out of the study and into the community to demand justice and participate in healing."[11] Second, religious communities must abandon any theology of ownership if they are ever to move from viewing domestic violence as a private issue to seeing it as a public concern. They must be willing to critique and abandon all accounts of creation that serve to condone and justify a system of violating gender relations. Third, pastors and preachers must seek to develop a concept of responsible adulthood.[12] The church needs to lead the way in developing theologies that challenge all understandings of dominant/subordinate relationality. Mutuality, accountability, and interdependence must be nurtured and given value. Violence in human relationships might continue to exist, "but such actions would be considered aberrations of adulthood, an unacceptable loss of impulse control, and would be subject to the scrutiny and judgment of religion and society."[13] Dismantling the complex and multilayered dimensions of a theology of ownership is an enormous theological and homiletical task. These assumptions keep preachers and religious communities unable and unwilling to call for greater individual and community accountability. At present, violence is silently accepted as normative in human life. Until violent behavior is seen and confronted as a profound distortion, there can never be corporate responsibility.

RESTORATION AND HEALING

Holding an individual accountable for violence done is a redemptive, saving activity as surely as the act of stopping the violence itself. A part of breaking silence involves directly confronting those who are perpetrators. Holding persons accountable is a critical part of our saving, redemptive work in the world. Preachers are in an important position within the church to call for the kind of confession and reparation that make for justice. Perpetrators of violence are held accountable when they are asked to acknowledge the violation that has occurred, when repentance and transformation are actively engaged in, and when some form of restoration of those harmed is enabled.[14] As mentioned earlier, a part of developing a theology of responsible adulthood might involve preachers explicitly and implicitly deepening the entire community's commitment to an accountability that involves just restitution for the victim and redemptive transformation for the offender.

The need for restoration and healing also demands that preachers and religious communities move beyond an intellectual understanding of violence into the heart of this pain and terror. Until every man can sensitively imagine what it means to live daily with the fear of being raped, and until every woman is "moved by the deaths of other women,"[15] the silence of male violence will not be broken and the magnitude of women's pain and fear will never be fully exposed. Restoration and healing call each of us into compassionate imagining and embodied resistance.

While writing this chapter I made two calls trying to locate the most recent statistics about woman battering and rape. I was given the number of a center in Washington, D.C. After I dialed the number, a woman answered the phone. I said, "Hello, my name is Chris Smith." The woman on the other end of the line asked, *"Are you safe?"* I could not speak for a moment; then I answered, "Yes." I asked my question, thanked her for her work, and hung up the phone. For a few moments I wept uncontrollably. My awareness was fundamentally changed by that woman's question. Until the people of God can feel and experience the power and pain of that one question, we will never find the courage to confront the misogyny that engulfs all of our lives in perpetual cycles of violence.

What Should We Be Noisy About?

═ John B. Cobb, Jr. ═

WE SHOULD, INDEED, SPEAK up! But what should we say? In his speeches, Martin Luther King, Jr., addressed people who knew that his message was true and right but preferred to stay silent so as to avoid the backlash against it. They had counseled patience for a long time. Silence and patience had made no progress. King rightly insisted that the time had come to speak out loudly and clearly.

Many see parallels between the civil rights movement and the present. For many of them, Trump is such a villain and such a threat that to speak up is simply to attack him or warn people about how dangerous he is. This attack is equally acceptable on all fronts. If Trump supports a policy, these people feel certain that policy is bad and worthy of opposition. The implication seems to be that we should all loudly support the pre-Trump situation.

This widespread attitude among "liberals" frightens me as much as Trump's heaping more wealth on the superrich while dismantling environmental safeguards and healthcare. I am appalled that because Trump calls for ending the villainization of Russia, liberals support intensifying that villainization. It does not seem to bother them that they have become the war party, serving the interests of the neoconservatives. A war with Russia would probably be the war to end all wars—and everything else as well. Is contributing to that possibility, even a little, truly less evil than what Trump is doing?

Trump seeks to reduce enmity, and the chance of war, between Russia and the United States, and his actions have given us the first hope in a long time for peace and, ultimately, reunification between North and South Korea. Trump has signaled to a progressive South Korean leadership that negotiation with North Korea is allowable. In this instance, I wish liberals had been silent. But in fact, they have been far from silent in their opposition. I would like to speak up loudly for peace, but my liberal friends seem to believe that supporting moves toward peace in Korea makes me a traitor to the cause, which is defined as opposing Trump.

I would be far more enthusiastic about speaking up for other causes. But which ones? I am glad to speak up for single-payer healthcare, but liberals warn that this is a divisive issue within the anti-Trump camp. Maybe after we get rid of him, they suggest, we can discuss it. But for now, they are content to celebrate the very problematic form of healthcare that Democrats achieved during the Obama administration.

I would be delighted to speak up against much of the Obama administration's foreign policy when Hillary Clinton was secretary of state. When the Honduran military overthrew Honduras's president, the United States worked to legitimize the junta. The military government the Obama administration supported made Honduras a dangerous place for ordinary liberals to live in. It drove many of them to seek a new home in the United States. American support of the Honduran military coup is one of the main reasons for the excessive number of Central Americans seeking refuge here.

But speaking up about that would be a criticism of Hillary Clinton and Barack Obama and would run counter to the vilification of Trump. I am glad to join the attack on Trump's immigration policies. But since Obama's policies were not very different, I would also be criticizing them. Since no satisfying policies are even on the table for discussion, I would rather focus on the American imperialism and global capitalism that are responsible for so many Latin Americans abandoning their homelands. But on this matter, I have more hope for Trump's ethnic nationalism than for the American exceptionalism and globalism supported by both political parties in the past.

By all means, let's speak up. But let's focus on the goals of peace, justice, and sustainability for the whole planet. Let's recognize that those goals are not currently on the political table. Let's ask how we might make them part of the discussion. That would mean calling for a political movement not controlled by the establishment.

Since what we need is very different from what we had under Democratic leaders, our speaking up would not be in defense of what they have achieved. For example, we need an agency that would truly protect the environment, not the recovery of what we had under Obama. E. G. Vallianatos, who served the Environmental Protection Agency (EPA) for decades, tells in *Poison Spring: The Secret History of Pollution and the EPA* how EPA leadership has become increasingly subservient to the chemical industry.

We need an economic system that serves the people and the environment, not the one that has concentrated wealth and power in fewer and fewer hands, and especially in financial institutions, for decades. Yes, Trump's changes made the situation worse. We need to oppose these changes not to defend what we had but to envision and pursue what we truly need.

I believe we should commit ourselves to a multicentric global situation. The United Nations originally expressed that dream. The

United States manipulated it into supporting a unipolar vision. But Trump's policies have (probably unintentionally) motivated the representatives of other countries to vote according to their own judgments on at least some important topics. The United States increasingly depends on its veto power in the Security Council to keep the United Nations from working against US interests. Trump's policies and rhetoric have ended the credibility of any fiction about the United States playing a mediating role in Israel and Palestine. Can we use these changes to move the world toward internationalism?

We should speak out against Trump for many things. We should have spoken out against Clinton and Obama as well. *But speaking against should always be in the service of speaking for.* The silence that most upsets me is our failure to share with the American public a vision of the world we need—a world that might still be habitable fifty years from now. On this issue, silence is certainly not the answer.

Why I March

⟹ Vivian Elaine Johnson ⟸

THE SOUTH AFRICAN ZULU folk song "Siyahamba" says,

We are marching in the light of God,
We are marching, marching,
We are marching, marching,
We are marching in the light of God.

The term *to march* often has a military connotation. For some, as in the song above, it has religious significance. To march is also a type of protest or demonstration in which people walk through a public place to express their support of an issue.

My first march "in the light of God" was in 1990, when I was in my fifties. My church in Minnesota held a march the Saturday before Mother's Day. Though historical reports vary, some say that Mother's Day began as an antiwar effort. (It soon morphed into a Hallmark-type holiday.) My church traditionally held a mothers' peace march every year in remembrance of the genesis of the holiday.

My seventy-seven-year-old mother visited my congregation that day, and I invited her to join us in the peace march. I was surprised when she accepted because she was a private person, not one to call attention to herself. Careful, gracious behavior was her style. Before acting, she asked, "What would the neighbors think?" Mother was a believing person, a church-going, mission-supporting, Bible-studying person of faith. Before acting, she asked, "Is this God's will?" She was a trusting person, a government-supporting, voting, law-abiding, patriotic citizen. Before acting, she asked, "Is it democratic?" Mother was a genteel person, with a wisp of a smile and two tender blue eyes peeking out from a puff of soft white skin, open to people around her.

Her attire belied her destination that day: A ribbon-trimmed, wide-brimmed hat accentuated her white permed hair. A crisp white suit with blue trim clothed her round frame. Whitewashed high heels completed the look. She looked like she was headed to a luncheon or a fashion show, but she was marching in a parade.

It wasn't much of a parade—only twelve marchers if you counted the baby in the stroller. My mother, the unlikely demonstrator, stood at the head of the parade, behind the police escort with his gaudy, blinking lights.

She shyly struck up a conversation with her marching partner. "My son went to war. When he came home, I said, 'John, you're so thin!'

"'Mom,' he replied, 'I've got my arms and my legs. I can see and hear. Just be glad I'm home.'" Mother's marching partner nodded.

Then, with steely resolve, Mother added, "We who raise children should *refuse* to send them off to war!"

A private person took a public stance that day. A believing, trusting, genteel person marched in her high heels right down Main Street. She held high a banner with large red letters: mother's peace march!

While I'm astounded that my mother marched, I must admit that I'm surprised that I did too. Like mother, like daughter? Neither of us are the marching "type," whatever that means. I think I felt that if Mom could do it, I could too.

So, why do I march?

- *I march to call attention to an issue.* I want to remind leaders and the public of the importance of making a change. Historical precedent demonstrates that speaking up and marching bring progress. Our use of fossil fuels contributes to climate change; because I care for and want to help save the only earth we've got, I march for environmental causes with the sign "green, not greed."
- *I march to educate and raise money.* I march to raise awareness about Alzheimer's disease and HIV/AIDS, two of the most dreaded diseases of our time. When people sponsor marchers, that money goes to fund research and services for people dealing with these diseases.
- *I march to encourage those who need change and to show solidarity with those who would benefit from change.* The LGBTQ community benefits when I march for them.
- *I march because many leaders and others in power don't initiate positive progress.* It usually starts with people on the ground. I march in CROP Hunger Walks because the world's hungry cry for food. We need to speak for them.
- *I march for those who can't.* I march for the young people who died in school shootings. My banner states "Bullets are not school supplies!" When I march to protect our earth, I march for those who can't: polar bears, bees, turtles, coral reefs, and all of the natural world.

- *I march to be assured that I am not alone—I am part of a caring community.* Our visible presence shows that others have similar concerns. In whatever issue we support, we find strength in numbers. Numbers show the importance of an issue.

- *I march because it is one thing I can do.* My wallet isn't bulging, which limits my ability to donate large sums. My speaking ability isn't great; my energy is waning. But I am capable of using my feet.

- *I march because time marches on.* Some issues can't wait.

History reminds us of the importance of standing up to the powers that be. In the late 1800s, laborers marched to protect the common interests of workers; this resulted in the formation of labor unions that achieved decent work conditions and wages, break periods, and a five-day work week as well as the outlawing of child labor. In the early 1900s, women marched for the right to vote. In the 1960s, people marched for civil rights; migrant farm workers marched to improve social and economic conditions and to fight discrimination; and marchers protested the Vietnam War well into the 1970s. All of these marches resulted in new legislation and positive change.

Though women finally received the right to vote in 1920, fifteen years before I was born, I'm still marching for women's rights. This year, in solidarity with the #MeToo movement, my sign said, "Our rights are not up for grabs, neither are we." You may roll your eyes and say, "Get a life, Vivian. You've got it pretty good." Yes, I've got it good. But am I my sisters' keeper? Any violation of my rights is relatively minor compared to the statistics in the United Nations report *The World's Women 2015: Trends and Statistics*:

- Women are two-thirds of the illiterate of the world.[1]
- Women are half of the poorest of the world.[2]
- 19 percent of US women are physically violated.[3]
- Women and girls are 49 percent of the world's refugees.[4]
- Women are 83 percent of domestic workers.[5]

Author Sue Monk Kidd wrote, "There is a time when you are simply seized by tenderness for the world."[6] She sensed this when she turned fifty and wondered if it stemmed from entering the second half of life and having children and grandchildren and therefore wanting to make a contribution to this world.

Her words resonate with me; I do feel tenderness for the world and all its people. Since my eightieth birthday, I've participated in five marches, even though I'm not the "type." Because of my tenderness toward the world, I plan to continue "marching in the light of God."

Emancipation

≡ Richard Rohr ≡

PERHAPS YOU MAY WONDER why we chose the precise word "emancipation" for our theme for this edition of *Oneing*, instead of the more common word "freedom." I take the risk of using emancipation in a specific way, to encourage us to think anew.

I will begin by giving you a dictionary definition of emancipation: "To be set free from legal, social, or political restrictions." Emancipation directs our attention to a systemic level of freedom rather than just the personal freedoms enjoyed by individuals. To move our attention to this deeper and broader level, I am using the term emancipation to refer to the larger freedom few of us enjoy, which is actually quite scary. With the exception of those who are fully emancipated, we each live inside our own smaller security systems, political correctnesses, cultures, and eras—quiet, even secret agreements that are "too big to fail."

Americans, for example, rightly revel in the fact that we enjoy certain rights and freedoms from restraints (free markets, free speech, and the freedom to be secure and defend ourselves). We typically pay little attention to the fact that these liberties ultimately depend on an interior freedom within oneself, and a total dependence on the system itself—which, paradoxically, can never fully guarantee or deliver these very freedoms. Our inability to recognize this has made our so-called freedoms very selective, class based, often dishonest, and open to bias.

For example, are we free to think or imagine that there could be alternatives to our free-market system? Largely, we are likely to be called dangerous or un-American if we dare broach the topic. We believe in free speech, but know better than to claim that money is actually what controls our elections, rather than "one person, one vote." How many of us feel free to publicly praise an island country like Cuba? Does our freedom to protect ourselves (gun rights and limitless military spending) give us the right and freedom to use the vast majority of the natural and economic resources of our country for our protection? Even if it means not providing food, healthcare, or education for the same people that we say we are securing? Do we even have the freedom to politely ask that question during the course of ordinary cocktail-party conversation? I think you begin to see how rare full emancipation might be; how we mostly talk only about the freedoms that exist within agreed-upon boxes.

Only citizenship in a much larger "Kingdom of God" is the antidote to confinement within those well-hidden, yet agreed-upon, boxes. In fact, because they are foundational and necessary cultural agreements, we do not even recognize them as boxes. When we place all of our identity in our one country, class, or ethnic group, we are unable to imagine another way of thinking.

To be fair, sometimes such boxes are good, helpful, and even necessary! These silent agreements allow cultures to function and people to work together. But my job, and the job of any spiritual wisdom, is to tell you that "we are fellow citizens with the saints and part of God's household" (Eph 2:19), and thus "our citizenship is in heaven" (Phil 3:20). We have been called to live in the biggest box of all, while still working and thinking inside of smaller boxes. That is a necessarily creative and difficult tension, yet it is really the only way we can enjoy all levels of freedom.

So we will use the word emancipation to describe a deeper, bigger, and scarier level of freedom: inner, outer, personal, economic, structural, and spiritual—all at once. Surely this is the task of a lifetime. Those who achieve this level of emancipation really are "from another world" and, frankly, disturb and irritate those invested in smaller security systems. Precisely because they cannot be bribed by its payoffs, punishments, and rewards, their insider/outsider status allows them to be fully and freely involved in this world. Their final and full freedom is that *they do not need to buck the system or see themselves as outsiders or mavericks at all.* They simply are.

Who Is Jesus for Us Today?

⟹ Wesley Granberg-Michaelson ⟸

OUR CONFESSION OF FAITH sometimes means resisting secular authority. This is such a time.

The forces shaping, and misshaping, the world today include chauvinistic nationalism, growing economic inequality, deeply embedded misogyny, destabilizing climate change, unprecedented forced migration, and increasing militarization and violence.

Crucial to our response to all this, however, is a fundamental question: Are we confronted today simply by another set of vexing economic and social developments that require our attention? Or is something deeper at stake? Are we facing forces that constitute a spiritual assault on the integrity and truth of Christian faith in today's world? Is this a time when our response, however well intended, will be inept unless it is grounded in a spiritual resilience that confesses faith in Jesus Christ, through the power of the Spirit, who unmasks and defies powers that would subdue and crush the public integrity of the gospel in the world?

This is, in truth, the crucial question for us to discern. And it is deeply serious. I'd pose it this way: When rising forces of nationalistic exclusivism are fueled by racial bigotry, when a naked global struggle for money and power shreds bonds of human solidarity, and when unbridled greed threatens planetary survival, is the truth and integrity of our faith at stake? Is the only response capable of addressing the roots of this crisis one of spiritual resistance and renewal rooted in what it means to confess Jesus Christ as Lord? In other words, is it a *kairos* moment calling us to a clear discernment of what it means, in this present context, to confess our faith? And must such a confession then shape the communities of those who believe the gospel? In my view, the answer is yes.

WHEN A SEMINARY BECOMES A THREAT

The most cogent historical lessons for framing the church's mission and witness in this time might be found in the soil and history of Germany where, of course, were birthed the passion, faith, and truth that propelled the Protestant Reformation. We recall the courage it took at Wittenberg to confess God's Word and Truth in the face of a prevailing system whose corruption seemed matched only by its unassailable power.

But also significant is the story of Finkenwalde. This city lies on the east side of the Oder River. Today it's in Poland, and named Zdroje. But before 1945 this was part of Germany, and Finkenwalde was a suburb of Stettin. It was here, in 1935, that Dietrich Bonhoeffer struggled to discern the shape and character of the church's mission and witness in the context where he found himself, during the rise of the Third Reich. He witnessed a nationalism that was becoming chauvinistic and exclusive, contaminated by racial pride and exploiting economic grievances through bigotry and rejection of those who were different. Political and economic power were married and harnessed to obstruct dissent and reinforce a mindset of cultural superiority in the name of rectifying national grievances.

In all this Bonhoeffer and others saw the established church as deeply complicit, functioning with inexplicable comfort toward this emerging order, whose values so clearly violated the message of the gospel. The conflict intensified as the National Socialist government moved to establish direct control over the "German church." This led to the Barmen Declaration, drafted primarily by Karl Barth and adopted in 1934, laying the theological foundation for establishing the Confessing Church, with the leadership of Martin Niemöller and other German pastors.

Bonhoeffer went to Finkenwalde in 1935 to start an underground seminary that would train pastors to serve in the Confessing Church. He perceived that established Christianity in Germany was failing the test of that time. It did not produce the depth of discipleship, the strength of commitment, nor the spiritual foundation deep and resilient enough to offer the witness that was required to face the fearsome idolatries propagated by an emerging evil empire.

In response, life together at Finkenwalde focused on building a Christian community capable of nurturing Christian faith that understood the cost of discipleship and nurtured the means for its practice. Students were encouraged to dwell in the Word, rest in prayer, support one another, and turn in solidarity to those most vulnerable in society. Bonhoeffer sought to create a Christian community capable of instilling and forming a depth of faith capable of resisting the onslaught of evil he saw arising in his country's life.

In 1937, the Gestapo shut down the underground seminary at Finkenwalde and arrested many of its students. Apparently, the authorities recognized the threat posed by those who simply read the Bible and prayed about the nature of God's mission in the specific context of their time. Dietrich Bonhoeffer continually asked this question: "Who is Jesus Christ for us today?" That question, asked at any time and accompanied by a clear discernment of the times, will undermine the power and authority of any regime intent on imposing a reign based on the prerogatives of privilege, race, wealth, and might.

FAITH WITH THE POWER TO CONFRONT

It is also our question at this *kairos* moment as we discern the shape of God's unfolding mission in today's world and our participation in this work of the Spirit. Asking this question drives us, like those at Finkenwalde, to seek those practices and form those communities whose life and work embody a faith with the power to confront and overturn the idolatries of this era. That rests on a resonant and fresh confession of our faith and propels us to embrace those ways of discipleship that can sustain our witness in the long run.

This requires far more than the right words. We know that words matter. But the danger is to believe that once we say it correctly, and get the words planted in our heads, then our hearts will automatically follow, shaping our lives.

It requires more than the persuasion of well-crafted words analyzing our present context and commending action to prompt participation in God's mission in such a time as this. This takes the unfettered allegiance of people's hearts and the formation of their lives of discipleship. Countless pernicious forces press in the opposite direction, lulling the church back into complicit comfort, condoning narrow, nationalistic loyalties, offering the subtle idols of personal success and material reward, and promoting forms of spiritual escapism. It takes spiritual resistance, nurtured in communities of faithful disciples, to confront and overcome those forces. That was Bonhoeffer's lesson at Finkenwalde and should be our own today.

I am not maintaining a simplistic parallel between the rise of the Third Reich and Adolf Hitler's attempts to directly suppress and subvert the church with political realities faced today. Times and contexts are different. But the similarities of forceful appeals to nationalistic chauvinism, racial bigotry, and cultural exclusivism as manipulative reactions to economic anxieties, particularly in the United States and Europe, are chilling.

What is parallel between that time and this, for all of world Christianity, is the call to freshly confess faith in ways that shape the church and form disciples with enduring capacity for the spiritual resistance, renewal, and transformation required for this moment in the world's history.

Our response to God's mission has its roots in communities of discipleship, expressions of the body of Christ in local congregations. It is here, in the congregations where you and I worship, that the shape of the gospel is to be seen and understood, in flesh and blood, by others. That's why it is said that "the local congregation is the hermeneutic of the gospel."

People don't just want to hear about faith. They want to see what it looks like in the communities of men and women who claim and are claimed by this faith. When participation in God's mission is placed at the heart of a congregation's life, the living God renews and transforms us. Yet God's mission is never something that the church confines and controls.

Thousands of congregations are struggling with the call to respond faithfully to the pernicious forces shaping so much of our world. But that can't be done in isolation. Just as individual members cannot live independently from others in a local church, congregations cannot thrive in their witness if they are isolated from others.

Could we imagine ways that take seriously congregational journeys in vastly different regions and situations that all strive for costly and faithful engagement in God's mission? Could we connect such congregations in a virtual electronic community, sharing and networking together, and answer from their own contexts the question, "Who is Jesus Christ *for us today?*"

FROM FRENZIED ACTIVITY TO BUILDING COMMUNITY

The church today faces the challenge of embarking on a pilgrimage, a journey from the necessity of words to the formation of lives, from the announcement of our declarations to the pronouncement of our discipleship, and from the frenzy of our activity to the building of Christian community.

This pilgrimage poses these questions along the way: Are we ready to live in our identity as a *communion*, expecting that we are covenanted together as communities of faithful discipleship obedient to the *kairos* nature of this time? Can we truly place our commitment to join in the movement of God's mission at the center of the church's life and identity? Are we willing to direct the church's material and spiritual resources toward learning from the practices at Finkenwalde and all the places like that today?

Can we nurture the formation of Christian faith in communities of missional discipleship that can stand the test of this time? And can this compel us to participate courageously and joyfully in God's reconciling and redeeming mission in the world? That is the pathway for the living God to renew and transform us.

Part II

Listen to Your Moral Compass

WE ALL HAVE A moral compass. Sometimes it is silenced by the clutter and controversy of so many social and economic issues. But deep down, we know what is right and what is wrong. There is a pathway that leads to life and freedom, but sometimes that pathway gets obscured or distorted. Our nation and the world need to listen once again to our moral compass. It lets us know when a change of direction is needed.

Religious leaders have a responsibility to remind people of their moral compass. This is called prophetic preaching. Bishop Herbert Chilstrom's published letter to an Arizona newspaper uses the example of the prophet Nathan confronting King David about committing adultery with Bathsheba and arranging the death of her husband, Uriah. It took great courage for Nathan to speak out, but he succeeded in getting King David to see that he had violated his own moral compass and repent.

Old Testament scholar Walter Breuggemann makes it clear that public preaching is done under the watchful eye of those who employ us and pay our salaries. The preacher also owes allegiance to another authority: Jesus. Sometimes these authorities conflict, and we must choose whether to follow the way of the world or the way of Jesus.

Pastor David Nagler shares his advice on the awesome task of being a preacher in today's troubled world. Pastors often find themselves following in the footsteps of the prophet Amos, who wasn't planning to be a prophet but nevertheless was called to speak out against corrupt, oppressive political and religious authorities. Prophetic preaching is not a commodity to be purchased at a bookstore or conference. It is becoming aware of the need to listen to one's moral compass in difficult times.

Theologian and activist Ched Myers demonstrates that even Jesus had to be reminded of his moral compass sometimes. When a Syrophoenician woman asked him to help her daughter, she broke the social protocol of her time. She was not a Jew, she was a woman, and she was an outcast, so Jesus had every reason to dismiss her. But when she said, "Even the dogs under the table eat the children's crumbs," she reminded Jesus that compassion is more important than honor and prestige. This is a powerful story that we sometimes dismiss because we are unfamiliar with many of its historical and cultural nuances.

The principles of right versus wrong and justice versus injustice extend beyond human society. Feminist theologian Sallie McFague draws our attention to the damage happening to our earth and the environment. Human behavior and practices are part of the problem. If we neglect the healing of the earth, we lose sight of our moral compass. The survival of all humanity is at risk. The good news is that we can do something to change this, but we must act soon.

A few years ago, I wrote a letter to my bishop that called for rethinking our theology and sacred practices. Sometimes our traditions and policies can become idols that are worshipped in and of themselves and can divert us from following our moral compass.

Does our current theology fail to emphasize love for our neighbors, the poor, and the oppressed?

It has been traditional to think of love as the central tenet of the gospel and to assume that working for justice should automatically follow, making justice secondary. I contend in another piece that justice is not secondary but is the essence of the gospel and needs more attention. We tend to forget that when we speak about God's love, we are talking about God's justice, about a right relationship, about changing structural evil. When justice becomes secondary in our proclamation of the gospel, we can lose sight of our moral compass.

Citizens were outraged when our government initiated a policy to separate migrant children from their parents, who were seeking asylum in the United States. When he learned of this, my pastor, Paul Tellström, didn't wait to see what others said. Instead, he spoke out about the sanctity of family. His voice, joined with others, made a difference. The government changed its policy, but we are still living with some of its ramifications. Once again, we learn that staying silent is not the answer.

Sometimes when we speak out about what we believe is right, our message receives pushback. Pastor Dan Roschke shares the questions and frustrations of those who have experienced this. Prophetic preaching should always be sensitive to those who disagree with us, but we should never allow them to silence us.

Following your moral compass can be difficult or even frightening—it's easier to just go with the flow and avoid the consequences of speaking your mind. As these writers show, however, there is strength in joining with others and standing in solidarity with the poor, the oppressed, and the marginalized.

Advice for Aspiring Preachers

⟹ David Nagler ⟸

THE CALL TO PREACH the gospel is a sacred and sometimes frightening thing. It requires a significant amount of self-reflection, an open-minded study of scripture, and an ability to discern the spirit of the times. You will get it wrong. There is no way to avoid that. You will say things that you will later want to take back. But you will also have moments when you experience the steadfast love of God and are inspired to preach true justice.

Good news! You are not alone. You have companions that span both the globe and the ages. Listen to them. Some of these brothers and sisters died thousands of years ago. They lived in a very different context from twenty-first-century America, but their core challenges may be familiar to you.

Take the prophet Amos as an example. Like most prophets, perhaps like you, he did not choose his job. His life plan did not include confronting the king and subsequently being ostracized by Amaziah, the priest of Bethel. Amos described himself as "neither a prophet nor the son of a prophet, but I was a shepherd, and I also took care of sycamore-fig trees."[1] In other words, Amos had neither the lineage nor the inclination nor the training to speak truth to power, but God evidently considered this humble shepherd perfect for the job.

That is important to remember. For Amos to do what he felt called to do he could not operate from a position of privilege. Unlike his counterpart, Amaziah, Amos's calling did not come with a salary or a retirement package. He had to be the champion of the minority opinion—which also happened to be the truth. That kept his ministry focused and pure.

You, on the other hand, have been called by the institutional church. You have a salary and a pension plan. That will muddy the waters at times because it is harder to speak boldly to the entity that also feeds and houses you. You will sometimes sense tension between the message of the Bible and the very human concerns of the institution. You will have to live with this tension as long as you represent the institutional church; but on the bright side, it can challenge you to speak creatively and clearly.

When you face a choice between what you believe God is calling you to say and what the institution would prefer you to say, choose the path of God every time. You won't always, and that is why forgiveness matters, but as a general principle, choose God every time.

You will know if God is calling you the same way that Amos did. You will hold up a plumb line to the society that you have been called to serve and ask a simple question: what would most benefit the poor, the outcasts, the despised, and the forgotten? Any "good news" that does not help the poor and vulnerable is not good news. It is propaganda intended to keep the people in power comfortable. It provides charity without justice. It offers no liberation to the people held in bondage to oppression.

If you are white, straight, well educated, economically advantaged, or male, then you have an unfair advantage that you did not earn but should not be ashamed of. It is simply the situation you were born into. Hating your privilege serves no one.

However, a great responsibility comes with this unearned privilege. You are to pour it out on behalf of those who do not have it. This means that when doors open for you, you need to hold them open for others who otherwise could not gain access. You need to cultivate friendships among the underprivileged so they can be with you in spirit in every meeting, prayer, and decision. Your job is to spend your inheritance, unfairly gained as it is, on bringing about a new world with a more equal playing field. That would be really good news for the poor. You can be part of that.

You may be tempted sometimes to preserve your own temporal comfort and gain praise by offering lip service to caring for the poor while failing to advocate for any real change in the status quo. The poor see right through this, and when they love you, they will tell you when you are doing it. Listen to them! People from diverse backgrounds have different perspectives that can help you discover your blind spots.

Always keep an open and curious mind. The shadow side of the call to prophetic ministry is the risk of becoming judgmental. Many social justice events are rife with judgment and almost devoid of curiosity and grace. There are real injustices in the world that break God's heart and will break yours, but it is important to ask why people with different opinions than yours think the way they do. You must try as hard as you can to understand their way of seeing and being in the world. To dismiss them as simply racist or selfish or, God forbid, evil is to compromise your own ability to effect change. To do so is to capitulate to the applause of those who share your opinion, and that stroke to the ego snuffs out the candle of curiosity.

Curiosity is the key to the future of humankind and the health of the planet. Dualistic thinking always results in winners and losers. It creates a world of victims and villains, good people and bad people. That is bad anthropology and definitely bad theology. Jesus points out that God sends sunshine and rain on the just and the unjust alike.[2] In reality, there is no clear separation between these two groups in the human family. We are, as Martin Luther points out, saints and sinners at the same time.[3]

So, when you find yourself getting understandably outraged by what you see on the news or hear in your congregation, pause for a moment, take a few deep breaths, and ask why. Why do they have that opinion or support that policy? How did they come to understand the world the way that they do? Do you share any points of agreement or connection with them?

This questioning should not happen just in your mind but also in person. This means that you have to interact with people who you may have initially categorized as enemies. You will hear and see things that offend you. When that happens, practice curiosity. The goal is not for you to compromise your values but to recognize the nuances of an issue and to build relationships.

Amos went to the temple in Bethel and to the king's court to speak up for the poor and the oppressed. He was part of a long line of prophets that seek not simply the destruction of the system and its perpetrators but the redemption of all God's children. When the systems of oppression fall, all are liberated, including those who thought that they were benefitting from the system but were in fact losing their very souls.

The biblical prophets stood in this line of loving truth tellers. Your social justice heroes were part of this parade. And now, so are you. God created you for this, and your community has affirmed your aptitude for this work. Remember that always because what lies ahead is not a well-trodden path. You are about to enter a wilderness because you have been called to serve in this time and this place.

May God bless you with joy, a healthy sense of humor, and love. Love God. Love yourself. Love your neighbor. Love your enemy. By doing so, you will fulfill your calling.

Appearing before the Authorities

⇒ Walter Brueggemann ⇐

I WANT TO THINK with you, dear sisters and brothers who preach, about the words you dare not speak from the pulpit, and what that "not daring" does to our hearts. Because when you preach, every time you do it, it is done as you "appear before the authorities."

I.

As some of you will know, George Carlin has a list of seven words you cannot say on television. He is as hilarious about the list as he is obscene. All of his prohibited words refer to bodily or sexual functions, the kind that cause junior high boys to giggle and blush. Carlin has a debate with himself about his list because some of the words are hyphenated and so reiterate others on the list. But when he gets the list set, he can recite it in two nanoseconds.

The reason Carlin cannot say these words on television is because the censors will not allow it, the censors being the guardians of establishment power to keep things nice and therefore safe. He cannot say these words because they remind us of bodily functions that we cannot control. We do not speak them because they remind us that we are bodies and therefore frail and therefore mortal and therefore about to die. Arnold Toynbee has said that death is "un-American," an affront to everyone's right to life, liberty, and the pursuit of happiness. The censors prefer matters nice and safe. They prefer that people like us talk of spiritual matters and not such topics as the body or the body politic or the economics of the body politic. The censored and disapproved list concerns the smelly and unsavory so that we do better to deny the body.

II.

Well, George Carlin is not the first to have such a list of things that could not be said in public. Already Jeremiah, in his frightened, jeopardized world, knew such a list of things not to be uttered in public in Jerusalem:

> He could not say that the divine promise to David was sheer ideology.
> He could not say that God's perpetual presence in the Jerusalem temple was a priestly hoax.
> He could not say that being chosen did not give Israel a pass on moral responsibility.
> He could not say that Nebuchadnezzar, the hated superpower, was a tool of God to bring it all down.
> He could not say that the Jerusalem network was under judgment and would not be spared or sustained.
> He could not say that God's eternity did not extend to the little human accomplishments that they loved too much with all their hearts. (Is that seven?)

He could not say these things, because he knew that saying them was inflammatory:

I am now making my words in your mouth a fire,
and this people wood, and the fire shall devour them.
I am going to bring upon you
a nation from far away,
O house of Israel,
says the Lord. (Jeremiah 5:14–15)

He knew he had to say these words because there were so many
false words that needed to be countered in Jerusalem:

Is not my word like fire, says the Lord, and like a hammer
that breaks a rock in pieces? See, therefore, I am against
the prophets, says the Lord, who steal my words from one
another. See, I am against the prophets, says the Lord, who
use their own tongues and say, "Says the Lord." See, I am
against those who prophesy lying dreams, says the Lord,
and who tell them, and who lead my people astray by their
lies and their recklessness, when I did not send them or
appoint them; so they do not profit this people at all, says
the Lord. (Jeremiah 23:29–32)

It was too dangerous to say what had to be said. And he did not
say it. And it tore his guts apart. He risked saying it, but at the last
minute he did not. And then he got sick for not saying it:

For whenever I speak, I must cry out,
I must shout, "Violence and destruction!"
For the word of the Lord has become for me
a reproach and derision all day long.
If I say, "I will not mention him,

or speak anymore in his name,"
then within me there is something like a burning fire
shut up in my bones;
I am weary with holding it in,
and I cannot (Jeremiah 20:8–9).

So finally he said it! He said it over and over! He was brought
to trial for his words, because the "spiritual leaders," the priests,
wanted him silenced for saying the prohibited words on television,
uttering the unutterable. In that trial he escaped by the skin of his
teeth because of some tough old witnesses who supported him and
who stood by him (26:17–19, 24). But he was regarded as a traitor
who "weaken[ed] the hands of the soldiers," that is, who "under-
mined the war effort" (38:4). It is no wonder that he cries out to
God in pain and anguish: "You have seduced me." You have given
me an impossible assignment. He prays in honesty for vengeance
against his adversaries. Because he had to say what he dared not
say. And all hell came upon him.

III.

Well, George Carlin is not the last one to have such a list of the
unsayable. There is, for example, you, you preachers who pray and
brood and study and know. And then mostly must retreat to the
"nice" of denial. Or you preach your heart out; and the vestry
or the session doubles the pain like a hammer, or a major donor
stomps out in indignation. Or worse, you preach your heart out
and the most you get is that someone reminds you that you forgot
the Lord's Prayer for God's sake! I am led to this thought by the
many preachers who have told me, almost in passing as though
it were normal, that they could not speak about the Iraq war in

their church or about immigration or about global warming. And I am, moreover, a member of a theological faculty that was not permitted to say something at the outset about the war because the institutional risks were too great! And my own daring preacher, on the Fourth of July Sunday, had a person walk out in a huff because he said something about US arrogance and privilege.

I have been thinking about a list of things, give or take, that a preacher cannot say. Or if said, is dismissed as a gal who never met a payroll:

Some could not say that the war is stupid, and we are expending our precious young on the folly of the national security state.

Some could not say that present day capitalism has failed in its excessive greed that devours the poor and now reaches into the middle class.

Some could not say that the oil spill is simply the token of Western technological hubris at its extreme.

Some could not say that we have forfeited our democracy to a secret government that runs over the Constitution and shreds civil rights in order to defend the intemperate wealth of the few.

Some could not say that the frantic rush to get a child to the next soccer practice and the next dance class is membership in the rat race that cannot be won.

Some cannot say that the technological fixes violate the neighborly fruitfulness of the creation.

Some cannot say that the immigrants are indeed sisters and brothers who come under the welcome sign.

Some cannot say that our penchant for violence is toxic to the heart of our common life.

Some cannot say that the experiment in greedy entitlement has
failed, and we will have to find other ways to maintain our
hummers. (Is that seven?)

Some cannot say things because the cocoon of denial claims us
all, and we would rather not risk so much. Well, maybe this is not
quite your list. You can adjust. All I know is that there is a lot not
being said, and we all know why.

This is not a sermon about being prophetic or taking on the
world or blowing the lid off the church in one loud binge. This
is a pastoral reflection on what it does for us, alongside Jeremiah
and George Carlin, to be silenced in ways that shrink and cramp
our humanness. Such coerced silence is not benign. It makes us
inordinately weary. It drives us to despair — or cynicism. It compels us to denial. It reduces us to managers and therapists and
cheerleaders and entertainers and program directors. And all the
while the word grinds at our guts because we know better. What
we cannot say is that the body is fragile and smelly and cannot
be made otherwise. What we cannot say is that the body politic
now has a smell of death about it. What we cannot say is that
evangelical faith is about bodily existence in the neighborhood,
bodily since the creator called it "good," bodily since God freed
the slaves from their pained bodily bondage, bodily since, as we
say in the creed:

For us and for our salvation
he came down from heaven,
was incarnate of the Holy Spirit and the Virgin Mary,
and became truly human.

Or as we know it more anciently, "and was made man!" Became human, fragile, vulnerable, smelly, about to die. Became man! When about to die, as "man" or as body politic or as us, then Carlin's "piss" or "fart" are not really objectionable or interesting because such smelly regularity beyond our control belongs inescapably to our short-term creatureliness.

IV.

Well, I thought it was worth reflecting on the fix we are in. The preacher in our society is given words that cannot be uttered. And if not uttered, the preacher grows cold, plays it safe, and perhaps needs to be loved more. And as I ponder this, I am aware that not once in my life, in my tenured life, have I been in the dangerous place that many of you occupy every week. You are like the apostles in the book of Acts, sure to be called before the authorities and examined for your testimony to see whether your words are safe and acceptable or as dangerous and inflammatory as those of George Carlin or Jeremiah. The authorities sit before you and conduct your trial.

But then I came to this other text given me by C. S. Song, the great Korean theologian, who has indeed been before the authorities. In Luke 21, Jesus anticipates the coming debacle. You wonder how he knew about our coming debacle: "Not one stone will be left upon another." It sounds like an oil spill or an economic meltdown. They asked him, "When?" He said, "I do not know." But then he says, before whatever time line in which it will occur: "But before all this occurs, they will arrest you and persecute you; they will hand you over to synagogues and prisons, and you will be brought before kings and governors because of my name. This will give you an opportunity to testify" (vv. 12–13).

They will ask you to speak up. They will expect you to utter your truth. They will watch your words to see if any of your words are like those of George's list or the list of Jeremiah. Then I thought, even if Luke is anticipating the Roman destruction of the Jerusalem temple, he is making connections to our time and place and danger. Now like then, the authorities are bewildered. They want some guidance or assurance for a dangerous time. So what do you have to tell us, Ms. Apostle, of the truth and nothing but? What have you got for us, Reverend?

And then Jesus says—or Luke says, or the Jesus Seminar says— these most stunning words: "So make up your minds not to prepare your defense in advance; for I will give you words and a wisdom that none of your opponents will be able to withstand or contradict" (vv. 14–15). Don't work it out logically and carefully or anxiously or with too much calculated caution, because that venue presses you beyond that. Trust the spirit of Jesus, he says, and receive wisdom that will admit you to new freedom. Imagine, on hard issues of the day before the Roman authorities, Jesus will be close at hand with a word. What he says is, "I will give you a mouth."

And then he says two things to his followers. First, this truth telling will get you into a lot of trouble: "You will be betrayed even by parents and brothers, by relatives and friends; and they will put some of you to death. You will be hated by all because of my name" (vv. 16–17). Second, you will be safe: "But not a hair of your head will perish. By your endurance you will gain your souls" (vv. 18–19). Big trouble . . . and you will gain your soul, your identifiable center of vitality. You will get yourself back in the process of telling the truth before the authorities. You likely will find allies among tough old witnesses. But for sure, you will have yourself in all your vocational freedom.

I do not give you advice. I give you only a text. I do know about the risk of the church budget and about the risk to one's family (I am a PK!) and about being without tenure and the danger to one's pension and medical coverage. Of course!

But I also know about the diminishment of self through coerced silence and the loss of freedom and courage and vitality and energy and joy. I crave for you an edge of freedom that will let you bear witness to the full truth that was entrusted to you. Jeremiah discovered, through his anguish, that he had allies as he ran risks, that he was kept safe in ways he could not have imagined. He could not know that before he bore witness. I have thought about what it means for us to walk close to the gospel. There is no doubt that great freedom for the word is needed among us. It is needed by those who need to hear. But it is also needed by those who are called to speak. This is a gospel time. This is a time when the old reliances have failed, when autonomous, arrogant ways of life, in many manifestations, have been shown to be empty. This is a moment to outline an alternative. We have that alternative, and it must be uttered for the sake of the body politic.

The utterance is not only for the sake of the body politic. It is also for the sake of our souls. Imagine what it will be like to break out of fatigue and despair and resignation and gentle denial to be one's self with the truth of the gospel. You do not need to be Jim Forbes, and I do not need to be Tony Campolo, with their bravado. We need only be ourselves with the word entrusted to us, with God's word given us, with news that sets us free from heart burn or ulcers or anger with Jeremiah.

The word we will be given in gospel freedom is not a nice word about a nice world. It is rather a true word about our bodies and our body politic, the bodies infused with God's truth, but none-theless temporary, passing, fragile, mortal.

All of us in his gathering are in it together. So I thought, let us together hold this moment precious. Let us think about the truth entrusted to us, the truth of God, God from God, true God from true God, the word that "was made man," suffered and died, and was indeed raised to new life and new freedom.

It is not a wonder that Jeremiah, at the end of his struggle with speech and silence, finally, in verse 13, breaks out in doxology:

> Sing to the Lord;
> Praise the Lord!
> For he has delivered the life of the needy
> from the hands of evil doers. (20:13)

He comes to joy by breaking his silence. I do not urge you to say more than you can say. I do not urge you to run risks in dangerous places that you cannot run. I do not lay a guilt trip on you. Rather, I invite you to take stock of the truth you have been given and to ponder what it would be like for you to move to greater freedom. Finger your head; check your hairs. Imagine them all counted and guarded and kept safe. Imagine the way the hairs on your head are safe and the way in which the freedom of your mouth is connected to the safety of our hairs. And then imagine, as your silence is broken, "Free at last, free at last, thank God almighty, free at last!"

Healing Political Bodies and the Body Politic*

⇒ Ched Myers ⇐

THERE IS AN ILL wind blowing across the land—and it smells like the subversion of democracy by plutocrats. In Donald Trump's America, economic and racial disparity are back on the rise. Just as troubling is the scapegoating and demonization of those who are still struggling to be fully included in American society— people of color, immigrants, the poor, and sexual minorities. Yet the privileged are disingenuously casting *themselves* as victims of social change and painting those who seek to bridge and heal social divides as dangerous, unpatriotic extremists.

We Christians know in our guts that categorical exclusion and *othering* is wrong, and that our churches are supposed to struggle against these forces in the name of compassion. But fifty years after the assassination of our country's greatest prophet, Dr. Martin Luther King, Jr., we seem to have forgotten *how*. We are inveterately timid in addressing social divides—we make vague allusions to the problem only to quickly soothe our anxieties with an empty rhetoric of

---

* This chapter is an edited version of a sermon delivered to Myers Park Baptist Church, Charlotte, North Carolina, on September 9, 2018; the Revised Common Lectionary texts were Prov 22:1–2, 8-9, 22–23; Ps 146; Jas 2:1–17; and Mk 7:24–37.

reconciliation that costs us nothing. Fortunately—or inconveniently, as the case may be—the Bible is far less polite, far less equivocal.

Proverbs 22 insists that rich and poor persons are equally valuable to God—which means the affluent should *not* be treated as more important. Proverbs also warns that social injustice inevitably leads to collective disaster and excoriates those who "rob the poor because they are poor."[1] These assertions are scorned by the Trump administration.

Psalm 146 states that God "executes justice for the oppressed; [he] gives food to the hungry. The Lord sets the prisoners free; . . . the Lord lifts up those who are bowed down; . . . the Lord watches over the strangers; he upholds the orphan and the widow."[2] Can we, as God's people, say the same about our priorities?

James 2 makes such matters uncomfortably relevant to our conduct and attitudes in church. James equates acts of social favoritism to functional atheism and asks why we Christians offer a warm welcome to the affluent but take pains to keep socially marginalized people at a distance.[3] The fact is, we middle-class folk demonstrate such discrimination daily—at church, at home, at work, and in our neighborhoods. We have things exactly backward—when we ignore the working poor, treat the homeless as if they were invisible, or criminalize immigrants, we disrespect those whom God specifically blesses. Moreover, we who despise downward while aspiring upward forget that it is the affluent who destroy the ecological commonwealth for profit, who litigate against the public interest, and who take the money and run. But our *worst* behavior is when we pray for the hungry or victims of abuse or people without healthcare but never manifest that concern as concrete acts of mercy or effective advocacy for more just policies. The only true solidarity is that which seeks to meet the bodily needs of marginalized people. No wonder historical church leaders as prominent as Martin Luther wanted to ban the dreaded book of James from the canon!

Proverbs, Psalms, and James all honor the Hebrew tradition of the year of jubilee, when slaves and prisoners were freed, debts were forgiven, and property was returned to the original owners. The jubilee tradition reminds us that persistent, structural social disparity is unacceptable to God and represents a reproach to middle-class churches in the United States, which have made their peace with social and economic inequality. We are practiced at holding the biblical ethos of equal justice at arm's length.

The question is, why *are* we privileged American Christians so ambivalent about the biblical insistence on a more just distribution of the gifts of Creation? Perhaps we are worried about what real personal and political change might cost *us*.

I believe that we Christians are so confused about social justice issues today because we've trivialized the significance of Jesus as a healer. Theological conservatives see Jesus's healings as miracles meant primarily to prove his divinity. Theological liberals, on the other hand, are skeptical of the supernatural elements in the Gospels' healing stories. Either way, we are missing the point: Jesus's healings are always about both bodies (which are always political because they embody how power and privilege are distributed in society) and the body politic.

In Mark's narrative, every healing episode represents an object lesson that illustrates a social problem. In a very real sense, the bodies of the sick people Jesus encounters mirror the social illnesses of the body politic that inevitably generate unhealthy persons. Jesus's healings thus always involve both the liberation of individual victims and a challenge to the *causes* of the disease. In this way, he is clearly operating in the prophetic tradition, which both advocates on behalf of the poor and strategically confronts those in power with the demands of justice.

Nowhere is this better illustrated than in Mark 7:24–30, in which Jesus journeys to Tyre, a coastal region northwest of Galilee that was considered outside the geopolitical scope of Judean society. There, Jesus encounters a Gentile woman—whose political body was completely othered by Galilean Jews—in an exchange that serves as a dramatic object lesson in radical inclusivity for the Jewish body politic.

The woman falls at Jesus's feet and appeals to him on behalf of her demon-possessed daughter. Because we are unfamiliar with the social norms of ancient Hellenistic society, we do not fully appreciate the scandal of this encounter. In the honor culture of ancient Judea, an unknown, unrelated woman approaching a man in the privacy of his retreat is inconceivable. Worse, she is a Gentile soliciting favor from a Jew. Mark describes her as "a Greek, born in Syrian Phoenicia."[4]

The fact that this interaction is an affront to Jesus's ethnic and gender propriety explains why he initially rebuffs the woman, which polite modern readers often find troubling even though we routinely do the same thing. Jesus is simply responding the way he is expected to as a Jewish male: he is rhetorically defending the collective honor of his people by putting the Syrophoenician woman in her place. Just ask people of color how often this happens to them in their daily lives.

Unfortunately, we cannot sugarcoat the fact that Jesus is *insulting* this woman. *Dog* was a popular Jewish epithet for Gentiles; a rabbinic saying of the time asserted that "he who eats with an idolater is like one who eats with a dog."[5] Exodus 22:31 commands that unclean meat should be thrown to the dogs. Jesus's stipulation that "the children be fed first,"[6] then, uses the table metaphor to assert his ethnic bias, which presumes that Jews have covenantal primacy. This is akin to the rhetoric of American exceptionalism that has been so militantly revived by the Trump administration.

Jesus probably expects that his conversation with the importunate woman is over—but it is not. This uppity woman boldly turns Jesus's eating metaphor back on him with this surprising and brilliant retort: "Lord, . . . even the dogs under the table eat the children's crumbs."[7]

Time seems to stop. Everybody freezes. Protocol has been strained to the breaking point. A Gentile woman has dared to challenge the rabbi and use his own words against him. Of course, she is only defending the right of *her* people to be included at the table. But from the male protagonist's point of view, she has gone too far. In American history, people were lynched for less.

Jesus looks at the Syrophoenician woman long and hard, feeling the indignation rise, assessing his options. But then, unaccountably, the man who bests every other opponent in verbal combat throughout the Gospel of Mark *concedes* the argument. "You know," he says slowly, "you're right. My bad."

This is more than a concession; Jesus responds with a wholesale *affirmation* of the woman's counterargument. "For such a reply," he says, "the demon has left your daughter."[8] The female outsider has enlightened the hero of the story. In the narrative logic of Mark, she has reminded Jesus of his own previous assertions that "nothing outside a person can defile them."[9] Jesus has been hoisted, so to speak, on his own petard.

Jesus's encounter with the Syrophoenician woman is usually interpreted one of two ways. Either Jesus admitted he was wrong or he allowed himself to be corrected to make an object lesson out of the exchange. Either way, the message is the same: Jesus's honor as a Jewish male is impugned by a Gentile woman who bests him. This, however, is precisely the problem with honor cultures then and now: they require winners and losers. Honor culture values underlie the current backlash against gains made by women and minorities and the vows to "make America great again." The story of the Syrophoenician woman models a different approach. Jesus's response to her appeal abandons both male prestige (his political body) and the collective honor of his people (the body politic) as the ultimate values to be defended. These are instead transcended by the value of *human solidarity*. This exchange between a Jewish rabbi and a Gentile woman radically redistributes race, class, and gender power.

Interestingly, Jesus's defense of Jewish primacy, "let the children be fed first,"[10] uses the Greek verb *chortazō*, which means "to feed, fill, satisfy." Mark uses that same verb in both wilderness feeding accounts, each of which conclude by saying all the people "ate and were satisfied."[11] The first loaves and fishes story takes place on symbolically Jewish soil, and the second one occurs on Gentile soil. This parallel suggests that Jesus is demonstrating the central principle of the divine economy: there is enough for *everyone*.

In his encounter with the Syrophoenician woman, Jesus models what we might call the cost of discipleship. But his short-term pain of losing face is eclipsed by the partial realization of the only goal that matters: the inclusion of *all* God's children in the kingdom of heaven. This story reminds us that only the human face and the pain of the other can help us see our own blind spots. Our personal and political health utterly depends on heeding the words of the marginalized.

From Mark's accounts of Jesus's healings, we can glean the following:

1. Jesus cares about both bodies and the body politic.
2. Jesus dealt with individuals *and* systems and with personal *and* public issues.
3. Somatic health matters; physical restoration is an essential part of the kingdom of God.
4. Underneath our physical ailments lurk deeper spiritual and social problems.

Denying people access, disregarding them, or treating them like they are invisible are all forms of exclusion in a body politic that marginalizes or dehumanizes certain political bodies. In 1955, Rosa Parks placed her body in a contested space and sparked a new movement in Montgomery, Alabama (where Martin Luther King, Jr., got his start as a civil rights prophet), and beyond. From the 1970s onward, disabled people struggled for the same rights of equal access, as many other groups in our society continue to do. When the church practices somatic faith, we stand (or sit) with anybody and everybody whose divinely created dignity is being compromised or suppressed. That is our ministry: not just affirming *private* rights but also *public* restorative justice.

Of course, when social boundaries are opened to include those previously excluded, the privileged in-group inevitably perceives itself as being diminished. We witnessed this in American history with the frustration of former slave owners in the South after the Civil War, which fueled a violent backlash to Reconstruction in the 1860s and 1870s and the proliferation of Jim Crow laws. A similar backlash to desegregation occurred a century later and continues today with the resurgence of the white supremacists.

But our history also includes a counternarrative not only of marginalized people struggling for justice and the preservation of their dignity but also of privileged white folks who recognized that when people of color assert nothing more or less than their equal humanity, it represents an invitation for whites to regain *their* humanity, which has been disfigured by ideologies of racial superiority. For example, Clarence Jordan, a radical Baptist from Georgia, got a degree in agriculture at the University of Georgia and a doctorate in the Greek New Testament at the Southern Baptist Theological Seminary—and then decided to found an interracial farming community in Americus, Georgia, in the 1940s! This was not exactly a great career move, but it transformed Clarence, and his Koinonia Farm experiment had an extraordinary impact on our churches. Even non-Baptists have been influenced by his *Cotton Patch Gospel.*

Eating plays a socio-symbolic role throughout Mark 6–8. The American history of social change also hinges on the act of eating. For example, César Chávez announced the end of his hunger strike in support of justice for farm workers in March 1968 at an outdoor Mass in Delano, California. Thousands of supporters attended, including the soon-to-be-assassinated Senator Robert F. Kennedy. César's deeply personal fast ended with a sincere public call for justice, read on his behalf by Senator Kennedy, that changed the struggle of low-income laborers forever.

Similarly, when four young African American college students sat down at a Woolworth's lunch counter on February 1, 1960, to order sandwiches and challenge the social protocols of a segregated society, they changed the world. Their sit-in rebooted a nonviolent revolution that had been brewing since Montgomery; within weeks of that protest in Greensboro, North Carolina, tens of thousands of young people—black, white, and brown—were sitting in all over the South and laying the groundwork for the next eight years of the civil rights struggle, which ultimately overturned the American apartheid. César Chávez and the black students at Woolworth's teach us that we should never underestimate the power of a strategic meal—especially when it defies boundaries.

Jesus models a Way that embraces the other and deconstructs one's own delusions of entitlement, all in pursuit of the kingdom of God that welcomes everyone to the table. Our pastoral and prophetic task as Christians is to help citizens anxious about preserving their privileges to see that true liberation lies in learning from the very people we fear or exclude or ignore. Risking communion with the political bodies of those we "other" is our only hope for healing our fragmenting body politic. Both the Old and New Testaments show us a way through the maelstrom of presumption and prejudice that swirls around *and within* us today, in which our collective insecurity is expressed through choruses to "build a wall," jacked-up defense budgets, and skyrocketing rates of incarceration.

Mark's account of Jesus and the Syrophoenician woman speaks to our need for deeper liberation. Jesus's initial dismissal of her tempts us to think that perhaps he was just having a bad day. But the question is not *whether* one is free of social prejudice but *how* one responds when that prejudice is challenged. This may in fact have been Jesus's finest hour because he showed us how to relinquish entitlement so we may bring about the kingdom of God. May we follow him in listening to and embracing the excluded so we *all* may be healed.

Living on this Planet so Others Can Live

≡ Sallie McFague ≡

MARTIN LUTHER'S UNDERSTANDING OF sin is a voracious, lustful desire to have it all for oneself, whatever "it" might be. From a twenty-first-century ecological perspective, "it" is refusing to share, refusing to live in such a way that others—other people and other lifeforms—can also live. In our time, sin is refusing to live justly and sustainably with all others on our planet, to share the banquet of life.

This is not a new understanding of sin; rather, it derives from the traditional view of sin being "curved in upon itself,"[1] as Luther put it, rather than being open to God. In our ecological age, we now see that being open to God means being open to the other creatures that we depend on and that depend on us. We cannot love God unless we love God's world. Christians have always known this because an incarnate God is a world-loving God, but now openness takes on new meaning and depth as we realize the radical interrelatedness and interdependence of all lifeforms.

To love God by loving God's world has meant different things to different people in different times. I suggest that for us today, it is epitomized by combatting climate change. Climate change is not just another social and political issue facing us—it sums up the central crisis of the twenty-first century. Put simply, climate change is the result of too many human beings using too much energy and taking up too much space on the planet. At over seven billion human beings, the planet cannot sustain the high-energy lifestyle that about 15 percent of us now enjoy and most of the rest of the world wants to enjoy.[2] Through our excessive energy use and the accompanying greenhouse-gas emissions, we are changing the planet's climate in ways that will make it uninhabitable for ourselves and many other species.

Environmentalism is not simply about maintaining green spaces in cities or national parks but about the more basic issue of energy use on a finite planet. Thus, space and energy, the basic physical needs of all creatures—a place to live and the energy to sustain life day by day—are the issues. Just as the Second World War was the quintessential issue of an earlier generation's day, so climate change is ours. During World War II, people all over the world mobilized, sacrificing their comfort and often their very lives, to avoid a threat of disastrous proportions. We face another such threat, one perhaps even more dangerous in terms of the long-term health of the planet, for it involves the very basics of physical existence—space and energy, habitation and food, clean air and arable land, and a viable climate in which life may flourish.

The crisis facing us is one of geography, of space and place and habitability, not time and history and human meaning. The threat of climate change is physical, earthly, worldly, and fleshly. Christianity often focuses on time, history, and human meaning; for example, salvation is traditionally understood as eternal existence in another world for individual human beings. But an incarnational Christianity, a Christianity that believes in an incarnate

God who loves and inhabits the world, is radically mundane. In Irenaeus's wonderful words, "The glory of God is a living man."[3]

Mankind living and living well on planet Earth in the twenty-first century is a doubtful prospect. If we continue living as we have been—and if more people join the high-energy lifestyle of us privileged ones—we are headed for disaster. Climate change is telling us loud and clear that the size of our population and our increasing excessive energy use are raising the temperature of the planet to the point where disastrous effects will occur: excruciating heat, melting glaciers, rising sea levels, violent storms, reduced arable land and clean water, declining biodiversity, more virulent diseases, and more wars fought over food and water.

This is a strange crisis to face: it does not have the immediacy of a war or plague or tsunami. Rather, it builds up according to how we live on a daily basis—the food we eat, the transportation we use, the size of the house we live in, the consumer goods we buy, the luxuries we allow ourselves, the amount of long-distance air travel we permit ourselves, and so forth. We are not being called to take up arms and fight an external enemy; rather, the enemy is the very ordinary lifestyle we are leading as well-off Westerners. And yet, for all its presumed innocence, this way of life, multiplied by billions of people, is both unjust to those who cannot attain this lifestyle and destructive of the planet that supports us all.

What, then, would be a good personal, professional, and public ethic for twenty-first-century people, especially well-off religious people? One of the distinguishing characteristics of many, perhaps most, religions is an emphasis on some form of self-emptying. This often takes the form of egolessness, the attempt to lessen focus on the self. From Buddhism's release of the self from desire through nonattachment to Christianity's admonition that to find one's life, one must lose it, religions are often countercultural in their ethic of self-denial in pursuit of genuine fulfillment. While such self-denial is conflated with asceticism and a retreat from life in some religious traditions, this is not usually the underlying assumption. Rather, one of the most basic religious questions—who are we human beings in the grand scheme of things?—is answered not by a narrow interpretation of individual desires but by relinquishment of being curved in on oneself in the service of a deeper and more profound desire.

We find ourselves by losing ourselves. That deeper desire is the desire for God, for nothing less will fill the hunger in us. Augustine says that we are drawn to God as a sheep is drawn to a leafy branch or a child to a handful of nuts.[4] To empty the self is not an act of denial but of fulfillment, for it creates space for God to fill one's being. We are satisfied by nothing less than God; our deepest desire is to be one with God, even as Jesus was. We were made in the image of God, and our destiny is to become one with God so that we too can say, "Not my will but yours be done." This is not a loss but a gain, the greatest gain.

Self-emptying is not an ascetic call to purify ourselves through self-denial or even a moral injunction to give others space to live but an invitation to imitate the way God loves the world. In the Christian tradition, *kenosis*, the Greek term for self-emptying, is a way of understanding God's actions during the Creation, in the Incarnation, and on the cross. During the Creation, God limited the divine self and pulled in, so to speak, to allow space for others to exist. God, the one in whom we live and move and thrive, does not take all the space but gives space and life to others. This is an inversion of the usual understanding of power as control; instead, power is given to others to live as diverse and valuable creatures.

In the Incarnation, as Paul writes in Philippians 2:7 (New Revised Standard Version), God "emptied himself, taking the form of a slave," substituting humility and vulnerability for cannibalistic appetites. On the cross, God gave of the divine self without limit to side with the poor and the oppressed. God does not take the way of the victor but, like Jesus resisting Satan's temptations, rejects absolute power and imperialism for a different way. Likewise, one understanding of Christian discipleship is that of a "cruciform" life that imitates the self-giving of Christ in our interactions with others.

What does all this suggest? What is this different way? We do not know for sure, but Christianity, like many other religions, is obsessed with the possibility of a better way of living in the world with all others. I believe the arcane and seemingly absurd notion of self-emptying may give us some clues for how to live in a time of radical climate change.

The kenotic paradigm is not simply asceticism or self-flagellation or a negative statement about the earth and life but the recognition that life flourishing on earth demands certain limitations and sacrifices at physical and emotional levels. The ego that demands everything for itself—honor, power, and money—is the same cannibalistic self that devours all the food and land. As Saint Francis well knew, possessionlessness is a matter of the spirit and the body: one cannot hold on to a sense of superiority while giving away all one's clothes to the poor. While self-emptying was viewed in other times as a peculiarly religious way of living in the world, I think it could be the germ of a new personal, professional, and public ethic for the twenty-first century.

Two factors characterize our time: first, an awareness of our radical interdependence with all other lifeforms and the vital climatic system of our planet; and second, an increasing appreciation of the planet's finitude and vulnerability. These realities of our time mean that the vocabulary and sensibilities of self-limitation, ego-lessness, sharing, giving space to others, and limiting our energy use no longer sound like a special language for saints but like an ethic for all of us. The major religions' intuitive appreciation for self-emptying and self-limitation could provide a framework not only for personal fulfillment but also for sane environmental practices. Could the major religions take the lead in exploring and illustrating how an ethic of self-limitation might function in the twenty-first-century crisis of climate change?

A Letter to My Bishop

≡ George S. Johnson ≡

AS WE CHRISTIANS THINK about the future and the opportunities that may arise in this *kairos* (meaning "opportune" or "decisive") moment, I wonder if it is time for us to *look at our theology*. Has our theology become a way to avoid addressing the crises our world faces today? Perhaps we should reexamine our approach to leadership, our educational programs, the needs and cultures of our neighbors, our worship and liturgies, and our resources and structures. As Douglas John Hall says, "The real crisis of Christendom as it encounters its own demise lies precisely in the poverty and inappropriateness of its theology. . . . We have all in some sense been seduced theologically by a history of intellectual and spiritual conditioning that is unbelievably hard to cast off."[1]

Are we too cautious about using the word *obey* nowadays? I wonder if our *emphasis on grace* has created an imbalance in our preaching and teaching, and as a result, the biblical call to love our neighbors and obey God has been silenced. Walter Brueggemann articulates this well:

The fearfulness and avoidance of obedience, as conventionally understood among us, has in my judgment two root causes, both of which are alive and powerful, even though not often frontally articulated.

The first dimension of the problem is the Augustinian-Lutheran dichotomy of "grace and law."[2]

In *God and the Excluded: Visions and Blind Spots in Contemporary Theology*, Joerg Rieger suggests that our current theology has *failed to include the poor*. He says, "Closer listening to the traditions and texts of the church from the perspective of the marginalized in light of God's own work will be the major task ahead for theological reflection."[3] Reiger goes on to suggest that we need to become aware of our theological blind spots and how we have been seduced into supporting a theology of exclusion by the powers that be. We need the courage to resist this. Dorothee Sölle reminds us that the poor are our teachers and that they are the ones who convert the rich and educated.[4]

I wonder if our theology has left us vulnerable to a kind of *individualism* and *nationalism* that promotes a piety divorced from politics. We shy away from the political implications of Jesus's teachings for fear of criticism. As a result, the prophetic voice of the church has been silenced not by any policy or careful selection of clergypeople but by a theology that is careful to avoid the economic and political implications of Jesus's teachings. Job security may be a factor in this silence.

Do our theology and proclamation of the gospel acknowledge the cost of discipleship? I don't think that Jesus waited until his listeners completely understood grace or reached a certain level of maturity before he told them that those who follow him will also have to take up the cross. Do we entice people to the table of Communion bread and wine without addressing the countercultural nature of our faith and the call to share that bread with the hungry? Do Christians understand that Jesus died not only for our salvation but also because of what he said and did? What does the cross mean today?

In *The Irresistible Revolution: Living as an Ordinary Radical*, Shane Claiborne describes how he became a Christian:

> I know there are people out there who say, "My life was such a mess. I was drinking, partying, sleeping around . . . and then I met Jesus and my whole life came together." God bless those people. But me, I had it together. I used to be cool. And then I met Jesus and he wrecked my life. The more I read the gospel, the more it messed me up, turning everything I believed in, valued, and hoped for upside down. I am still recovering from my conversion.[5]

Claiborne then goes on to say, "Charity wins awards and applause, but joining the poor gets you killed. . . . People are not crucified for helping poor people. People are crucified for joining them."[6]

This is not a call to completely abandon Lutheran theology, but as Martin Luther demonstrated with the *Ninety-Five Theses*, the church always needs to reexamine and critique itself.

Sanctity of the Family

⪦ Paul Tellström ⪧

FATHER'S DAY IS A day to remember what it means for a child to have someone to look up to and a day to protect that child within a family, however that family is made. Less than a week before Father's Day 2018, a horrific story chronicling the tearing apart of migrant families at the border appeared on the news, complete with photos.

I vividly recall some of the awful clips showing boys being taken from their fathers' embraces and infants torn from their mother's arms. I saw women and children put in cages—not "detention centers," but cages.

We're better than that. It can't be possible that we have lost our sense of empathy so completely that we cannot imagine what it must be like to take our children and escape the kind of violence that is happening in Central America, and in many other places as well. These migrants aren't coming to "steal our jobs." These families are escaping a vicious cycle of violence and death.

When our former attorney general, Jeff Sessions, quoted Romans 13:1–7 to justify taking children from their parents, many of us who speak from pulpits knew we needed to present a refutation of Sessions's interpretation of this passage. I know that those seven verses were read in many pulpits on Father's Day morning, including mine, and we talked about the context in which these verses were written:

> Let every person be subject to the governing authorities; for there is no authority except from God, and those authorities that exist have been instituted by God. Therefore whoever resists authority resists what God has appointed, and those who resist will incur judgment. For rulers are not a terror to good conduct, but to bad. Do you wish to have no fear of the authority? Then do what is good, and you will receive its approval; for it is God's servant for your good. But if you do what is wrong, you should be afraid, for the authority does not bear the sword in vain! It is the servant of God to execute wrath on the wrongdoer. Therefore one must be subject, not only because of wrath but also because of conscience. For the same reason you also pay taxes, for the authorities are God's servants, busy with this very thing. Pay to all what is due them—taxes to whom taxes are due, revenue to whom revenue is due, respect to whom respect is due, honor to whom honor is due.[1]

The problem with interpreting passages such as this is that while early followers of Jesus understood Romans 13 as outsiders to Rome, American Christians today don't realize that we have become Rome. We are the most powerful nation on earth—we can't escape the parallels. We interpret this passage through the eyes of privileged insiders and therefore turn the words of our faith back onto "the least of these."[2] The fact that we do this without self-reflection makes it even worse.

In *The First Paul: Reclaiming the Radical Visionary behind the Church's Conservative Icon,* authors John Dominic Crossan and Marcus Borg have this to say:

[Paul's letter to the Romans] was written in the mid-50s during the rather disturbed context after the death of Claudius and the ascendancy of the teenaged Nero. Its general, opening statements were intended to ground its specific, closing statements about taxes and revenues. It intends, in other words, to avoid martyr-dom for wrong or inadequate reasons.[3]

Borg and Crossan argue that Paul builds a case for quiet resistance in Romans 13. In Romans 12, Paul writes, "Bless those who persecute you; bless and do not curse them."[4]

How can any follower of Jesus tolerate the tearing apart of migrant families? Attorney General Jeff Sessions is a member of the United Methodist Church, yet he cherry-picked a Bible passage written during the rise of Nero to justify removing the protected status of children flee-ing violence.

In a statement from Rev. Susan Henry-Crowe, general secretary of the United Methodist Church, the denomination described these poli-cies as a "shocking violation of the spirit of the Gospel." She elaborated further on this theme:

The ethical teachings of Romans 12–16 describe that consecrated Christian life requires the duties of love and hospitality. The com-mandment in Chapter 13 to "be subject to the governing authori-ties" is bracketed by preceding and following passages containing the command to "love."

Earlier verses detail what love looks like:

> Let love be genuine, hate what is evil, hold fast to what is good; love one another with mutual affection; outdo one another in showing honor. Do not lag in zeal, be ardent in spirit, serve the Lord . . . *extend hospitality to strangers* (Romans 12: 9–11, 13 NRSV, emphasis added). . . .

> Jesus is our way, our truth, our life. The Christ we follow would have no part in ripping children from their mothers' arms or shunning those fleeing violence. *It is unimaginable that faith leaders even have to say that these policies are antithetical to the teachings of Christ.*[5] (emphasis mine)

It all comes down to this principle: love God, and love your neighbor as yourself. But once again, scripture was misused and abused to justify policies that oppress or harm children and families. If only Jeff Sessions had read just two verses ahead, he would have ended thusly: "Love does no wrong to a neighbor; therefore, love is the fulfilling of the law."[6] Paul reminds us that love is the way. Walking with Jesus is our way.

Those who use the Bible to justify these horrific policies should also read the words of the prophet Isaiah: "Woe to those who make unjust laws, to those who issue oppressive decrees, to deprive the poor of their rights and withhold justice from the oppressed of my people, making widows their prey and robbing the fatherless."[7]

Who are you to dismiss your own voice as too small to stand up for families that are being torn apart? Who are you to think that you cannot make a difference? Who are you to think that the seeds of new thinking, new life, and new being could not change your life and the lives of others?

Let your face reflect the love that we call God. The process by which the way of this world becomes the way of God is very slow, and that exasperates us. In the parable of the mustard seed, Jesus simultaneously cautions us to be patient and encourages us, small as we feel, to keep telling stories of injustice until people hear and understand.

Be a voice. Decent people don't turn a blind eye to people fleeing violence. Be a voice. Decent people don't put children in cages like animals. Be a voice! Decent and forward-looking people don't dispense cruelty to refugees from violence but seek a solution to that violence.

The parable of the mustard seed informs us that through love, we have the power to change the world. Romans 12–15 speaks of the kind of love that can overcome hate or injustice—so long as we don't carve out those seven verses that tell us to obey Rome.

A quote commonly attributed to Gandhi says, "Be the change you wish to see in the world." The power to do so is already within you. Even the smallest seed, once planted, can grow.

The terrible story of migrant families ripped apart came out after Mother's Day and right before Father's Day. Be the dad who would want the best not only for your own child but also for the kids who were torn from their parents. That's the kind of dad I would look up to. Likewise, be the mom who could not fathom what it would be like to lose one's child after coming so far in search of safety. You have power. You have purpose. Stand your ground.

When Prophets Confront Kings

⇒ Herbert W. Chilstrom ⇐

A SPOKESPERSON FOR THE so-called evangelical conservative community was interviewed recently on the PBS *NewsHour*. He's an occasional guest at the White House.

When pressed about President Trump's personal moral behavior, he responded with only the most oblique concern. He suggested that the reason so many in his community support the president is because of his stance on "religious liberty" and "respect for the sanctity of human life."

It's not difficult to understand that the issues he undoubtedly had in mind regarding "religious liberty" are prayer in public schools, prayer at major athletic events, freedom for business persons to refuse to serve homosexual persons, and more.

"Sanctity of human life" is obviously a reference to support for more stringent abortion legislation.

Combine this with such things as the apparent strength of the economy, tax relief for some Americans, and hopes for Mr. Trump's conversation with the head of North Korea, and it's not difficult to understand why support for the president remains surprisingly strong with some Americans.

But now let's step back almost 3,000 years. Visit Israel in the time of King David. Yes, as in the United States today, the poorest were being neglected and wealth was unevenly distributed. But, also like the United States today, the economy in Israel was strong, unemployment was low, the military was the most powerful in the region, and the borders and influence of Israel had never been so extensive.

Indeed, King David was very popular with many in the nation.

One man saw things differently. His name was Nathan. When power and wealth went to King David's head, he thought he could have anything he wanted, including the beautiful Bathsheba, wife of Uriah, an ordinary soldier. After he impregnated Bathsheba, David tried to cover his tracks by having Uriah killed in battle. Now he had a legitimate right to take Bathsheba as his wife. Or so he thought.

Not knowing the intent of Nathan's request for an audience, David welcomed him to his palace—Israel's "White House." Like American presidents over the past half century, David no doubt thought it to his advantage to curry the favor of prominent religious leaders.

But Nathan had something else in mind.

He told David a simple story about a rich man who saw a prize lamb in the backyard of a poor shepherd. In fact, it was the pauper's only lamb. When the poor man refused to sell it to him, the rich man arranged to have him killed.

On hearing the story, King David flew into a rage. He declared that the rich man must be executed.

At that moment Nathan riveted his eye on David and declared, "*You* are the man!"

What about modern-day prophets? It's my strong impression that very few of them, especially in the so-called evangelical conservative community, have the courage to raise a prophetic voice of judgment.

With our president's own recorded comments about his immoral behavior and after the number of women who have brought accusations of sexual misconduct against him, is it not reasonable to ask a few questions?

- Were he a teacher of our children, the head of a school system, the CEO of a television network, the mayor of a city, or the spiritual leader of a religious community, would he still be in office?
- What kind of example is he setting for all of us, and especially for our children?
- In his role as Commander in Chief of our military forces, is he the role model they should have?
- Are there some things, such as honesty, personal integrity, and moral rectitude, that are at least as important as a president's stance on religious liberty and sanctity for human life?
- How long can this go on without consequences for all of us?

This is not merely a political issue. Two decades ago, when Bill Clinton, a Democrat, marred the office with similar behavior, I wrote an opinion piece for the *Star Tribune* in Minnesota. I suggested several reasons he should resign. Would the country have collapsed had Mr. Clinton done so, or been removed from office? Of course not.

Would it happen if Mr. Trump did so, or was removed from office? Of course not.

We are a nation of a Constitution and laws, not of men and women.

Pastors Who Feel Trapped

== Dan Roschke ==

AS A YOUNG PASTOR, I must be honest and confess a spirit of
fear and trembling when it comes to preaching about *mishpat* and
saedekah (justice and righteousness). God siding with the poor, the
hungry, the convicted, and the undocumented—and calling us to
do likewise—doesn't always sit well with many in the pews. Even
though I am convinced that this is what I am called to preach,
in the interest of my job, my family, my pension, and my need
to be liked and affirmed, I sometimes take a less confrontational
approach. Here's where I might be rationalizing: In seminary, I
was constantly reminded of the importance of "meeting people
where they are," and in my first call, I learned what happens when
you don't. Walls go up, ears and minds close, and people shut you
down with sarcasm or they just plain avoid you—or at least avoid
any potentially sticky conversations with you. Achieving the kind
of intimacy needed to grow a heart yearning for justice is halted
dramatically.

So here are my questions.

To the wise older pastors, those of you who have been out there
preaching and acting out *mishpat* and *saedekah* for decades—can
you relate to my fears? How did you cope? What did you do if and

when people shut down? What mistakes did you make? And what has worked?

To the energetic young pastors, those of you who, like me, are in the early years of your ministry, passionate about peace and justice work and passionate about changing systems in the church and in the world that entrap the marginalized—what do you say and do? Do you, like me, feel trapped?

Why Justice Is Not Secondary

≡ George S. Johnson

THE BIBLICAL TERM *JUSTICE* needs our attention. It has become very popular—we hear about racial justice, environmental justice, economic justice, gender justice, global justice, and creation justice. But what do we mean when we use this word? What do people think and feel when they hear the word *justice*? We need to unpack this concept.

A review of the context of Reformation theology reminds us that fear of God and eternal damnation were dominant themes in European society in the sixteenth century. Works righteousness was strong in medieval Christianity, but grace, the unmerited love of God, became central to Protestant theology during the Reformation. Has our fixation on grace allowed justice to become secondary?

Our context today is different. Damnation is not our primary fear. Perhaps inequality, injustice, and violence are more dominant concerns in our time. What is good news in our context? By elevating grace above justice, have we missed something important in biblical theology? Grace is by no means secondary, but neither is love of one's neighbor. How do we integrate the two?

Was not love of one's neighbor central in the teachings of Jesus? Did Jesus ever suggest or act as though justice was secondary? Have we assumed that those who experience forgiveness will do justice? Is there a cause-and-effect relationship between our understanding of faith and our ethics that merits reflection? Asking who our neighbors are is part of justice.

The biblical terms *mishpat* and *saedekah* (justice and righteousness) almost always center on love of one's neighbor and correcting oppression. Justice is more than charity or relieving pain; it includes the elimination of the causes that bring inequality and pain. If we truly want justice, we must be willing to let go of privileges, systems and policies that contribute to the pain and suffering of our neighbors. Marie Augusta Neal's book, *The Socio-Theology of Letting Go*, is helpful on this topic. In what ways does justice include the courage to let go? Nobody wants to lose one's job or friends or pension. How do we help people in danger of such loss?

Responding to the biblical summons to seek justice and correct oppression is not easy and can be dangerous. Shane Claiborne reminds us that "charity wins awards and applause, but joining the poor gets you killed."[1] Dom Hélder Câmara used to say, "When I feed the poor they call me a saint. When I ask why so many people are poor they call me a communist."[2] Jesus reminded his audience of what happened to the prophets when they called for justice: "Blessed are those who are persecuted for righteousness' sake."[3] How can we help people understand this dimension of doing justice?

José Porfirio Miranda was well known for asserting that God can be known only through love of one's neighbor. How do we respond to this idea? In 1 John, we learn that whoever loves is born of God.[4] How do we interpret and apply that?

Rolf Knierim, my former Old Testament professor at Claremont School of Theology, taught me that worship was the primary setting in which ancient Israel experienced and celebrated justice. The advancement of justice and the proclamation of justice were the very function of worship. The psalms document this clearly. What is the role of justice in our worship today? Music is important. How do our liturgies, anthems, and hymns enable us to proclaim justice? Should an understanding of biblical justice be a consideration when hiring a director of music?

We hear more about justice today than we used to. Church schools and seminaries have found ways to include justice in their curricula and are making an effort to include experiential learning opportunities in the fields of social analysis and social justice. My alma mater, Luther Seminary in Saint Paul, Minnesota, has an endowed chair for justice and Christian community. Churches have formed committees to help members connect their faith to current issues of justice. All this gives me hope that we will stop putting justice second.

Part III

Your Voice Can Make a Difference

IT IS SO EASY to think, "My voice will not carry much weight. Who will listen to *me*? I have written letters and spoken out, but that hasn't brought about change."

My friend Bishop Lowell Erdahl, author of *Pro-Life/Pro-Peace: Life-Affirming Alternatives to Abortion, War, Mercy Killing, and the Death Penalty*, shares a list of ways individuals can break the silence and work for change. Not everything he suggests will work for you personally; you can't do everything, but you can do something.

Cultural values can change when people become better informed. Most churches initially rejected LGBT people, but when people had the courage to come out as gay, lesbian, or transgender, it made a difference. Pastor Brenda Bos paints a vivid picture of the LGBT community's struggle to be accepted. It took a while, but today, gays, lesbians, and transgender people are welcomed and their gifts appreciated in many churches.

Retirement is an important time to continue making a difference. Vivian Johnson shows that aging need not diminish one's involvement in the community even when one has physical limitations. Older Christians have the opportunity and responsibility to teach the next generation how to bear prophetic witness on behalf of the marginalized.

The biblical story of Jesus in the temple at age twelve suggests that sometimes we need to free ourselves from old patterns and practices. Pastor Paul Tellström calls us to push for change by practicing constructive disobedience.

Larry Rasmussen, Professor Emeritus of Social Ethics at Union Theological Seminary in New York, uses a biblical parable about trying to put new wine into old wineskins to point out that we are facing new realities and scientific discoveries that don't fit the old wineskins of our current living patterns. We face new challenges that require new wineskins. Climate change is a wake-up call to this reality.

Jim Wallis is an evangelical pastor and journalist who founded *Sojourners* magazine. His monthly editorials are a clarion call for evangelical churches and for all people to speak out and create change. Wallis argues for resistance to all forms of voter suppression. A biblical mandate (not just a suggestion) says "let your light shine before others, that they may see your good deeds and glorify your Father in heaven."[1] Your voice joined with others can make a difference.

You never know when your actions will become a spark that causes others to join the choir of protest. There are numerous examples of this. I attended a series of workshops in Los Angeles led by Dr. James Lawson, a Methodist pastor, on the power of soul force and nonviolent action exemplified in the life and ministry of Dr. Martin Luther King, Jr. My friend Ashley Herndon, who took copious notes, wrote a summary of his lectures. Lawson often spoke about the impact of Rosa Park's refusal to take a back seat on a bus, which sparked the civil rights movement. She had no idea that her one simple action would have such soul force. Gandhi's march to the sea was a protest to the British government. It started small but grew to thousands of participants. It too made a difference.

To speak out and stand up for what you believe is right is an act of courage and an expression of love in action. "The Shakertown Pledge," originally created and signed by a group of social justice advocates on retreat near Shakertown, Pennsylvania, is a way to hold ourselves accountable and motivate ourselves to act on our beliefs.

According to Christine Smith, author of *Preaching as Weeping, Confession, and Resistance: Radical Responses to Radical Evil,* one of the most powerful messages we can preach in the face of intolerance, discrimination, and exclusion is that of grace. When we preach—and more importantly, practice—grace, we demonstrate God's love to *all* people, even those on the margins of society, and we move toward a more equal and just world.

The writers in this section offer many ways for you to make a difference, including making a pledge, protesting, civil disobedience, and passing your experience on to the next generation. This is merely a jumping-off point—can you brainstorm additional ways to make your voice heard?

The Prophet

⇒ Vivian Elaine Johnson ⇐

THE OLD MAN INCHES his way to the pulpit. It's a long journey, and the congregation is holding its collective breath, but he makes it. All eyes focus on him as he reads the words of the prophet Isaiah. This old man reading from a script enlarged for his dim eyes was once an intense, fiery-eyed prophet himself. His voice, once a cannon in the pulpit, now shakes a little. After he concludes the reading, his weakened body and voice step aside.

A young family enters the pulpit. The bright-eyed toddler boy, held in his mother's arms, adds his thin, high voice to his mother's as she speaks into the microphone. His big sister hops around her parents' legs in a disheveled angel costume. Are they two prophets in the making? Their energy is a sharp contrast to that of the aging prophet—the old and the young, the bookends of life.

With assistance, the old man returns to his seat. I look at him through eyes blurred by rivers of tears and whisper in his ear, "Good job, honey." It reminds me of my comments to our children after a performance. As we leave the church, many people approach him and repeat my words: "Good job." Others say, "It was good to see you in the pulpit again." Yes, it was. He had prepared for this responsibility by rehearsing numerous times at home and in the car on the way to church that morning. In rehearsal, his speech was garbled by Alzheimer's at times—but not in the pulpit!

In our usual end-of-the-day routine, I ask him, "How was your day today?"

The tired but pleased old prophet responds, "I was in the pulpit today. It was a good day."

For me, the prophet's wife, it was a day when the sorrow of Alzheimer's was touched by joy!

A few weeks later, the old prophet says, "I feel so sad" as he limps across our living room and carefully deposits himself into his favorite chair. "I feel so sad," he repeats. "This is a sad day today. These books are my dear friends. My history. My journey. They're a part of me." Today is the last big purge of the prophet's tools: his cherished library. Yes, he gave away a few books every time we moved, but this time, he is clearing out almost all of them and saving only a couple dozen for himself.

We load the dear friends into a laundry cart and a suitcase, both with wheels, because the prophet has an idea for potential new homes for them. The physical and emotional fatigue take a toll; the prophet needs a nap. As he sits on the edge of the bed, he looks at me, his eyes weary, and says once again, "I had to say goodbye to some very dear friends today."

The prophet's idea for new homes for the books is carried out the next day. George has invited fourteen younger clergypeople and lay leaders to gather for a discussion in our apartment building's community room. They come from San Diego to the south, Thousand Oaks to the north, Redlands to the east, and everywhere in between. We sit in a circle as George begins our conversation by asking what books we are reading. Next, he segues into his main topic: breaking the silence as an urgent prophetic task of the church.

Several themes emerge in the course of our discussion. We decide that being prophetic is not a mere choice for the clergy but a calling. The attendees identify people they perceive as prophets today. They discuss how the establishment tries to silence contemporary prophets. They ask if the church is complicit with the government. They identify topics of justice that we must support and courageously speak out about. They affirm how important retired clergypeople are in the community of silence breakers.

We all enjoy the wonderful camaraderie, the respectful atmosphere, mutual encouragement, and a stimulating conversation that leaves the attendees with new ideas and the courage to become the prophets they feel called to be. Our time together concludes with lunch, but it is obvious that no one is eager to leave.

As for George's books, they are spread out over tables, the piano, and a credenza so the attendees can peruse them and choose any they want. I think they love that George underlined key phrases and made notes in these books; they view a *used* book as a keepsake from him. George has an easier time saying goodbye knowing that his beloved tools of the trade are going to good homes.

The next day, George writes an email to the attendees:

What can I say? Words seem inadequate to express how happy and blessed I feel after yesterday. Each of you participated so well. Time went by so fast. I still lay in bed thinking of all the good comments and questions that were so provocative . . . It would be great if more progressive thinkers could feel the energy felt in that room yesterday.

We receive numerous emails of gratitude for hosting the gathering.

As for me, I am left with an overflowing heart from all the people who expressed appreciation for George's prophetic ministry. I learn once again that old age can be difficult, but it can also be beautiful.

What One Person Can Do

⇒ Lowell Erdahl ⇐

EVERY REVOLUTION IN HUMAN history started with one person. Ancient customs like slavery, hostility between Christian denominations, and male dominance held sway over millions. Then one individual began to question, doubt, and disbelieve. Others followed and began to act in new ways. They were considered heretical, impractical, unpatriotic, irresponsible revolutionaries. But one day, after years of seemingly futile struggle, enough people tipped the scales for a new idea to transform an entire community.

None of us can do everything, but each of us can do something. We can invite others to join us, and as the movement for life grows, we can have a united impact far beyond what any could achieve alone. You may feel that your influence counts for nothing, but your voice may be the one that tips the scale, brings peace to the world, and replaces the institutions of death with institutions of life.

ACQUIESCENCE OR ACTION?

We can imagine that we would have been courageous in opposing the Inquisition, child labor, slavery, and the Holocaust, but today's issues aren't as clear when we are in the midst of them. We don't like what is happening, but we fear controversy and keep silent.

Millions have risked their lives in warfare, but how many of us are willing to risk even our reputations by working for peace and life in fullness for all God's children, including the unborn, the disabled, the infirm, people from other cultures, and prisoners on death row? By passive acquiescence, we affirm the institutions of death.

What is needed to motivate us to live as courageous stewards of life? Do we need to wait for more abortions and executions? Do we need an accidental nuclear explosion or even a "little" nuclear war to shock us out of psychic numbness and into sufficient revulsion to reverse the arms race?

It used to be said that alcoholics had to hit bottom before they came to their senses. Now we know that they only need to see bottom—that is, to recognize the coming, but still avoidable, catastrophe before experiencing it. Does a world drunk on national pride, intoxicated with military power, and overindulging in the other institutions of death need to hit bottom before we come to our senses? Haven't we enough sense and sanity to see bottom and choose new roads that lead to life?

While there is life, there is hope. Nuclear winter has not yet gripped our planet. There is still time to abolish the institutions of death. God is with us, empowering us through the Holy Spirit to work for the fulfillment of life. As John 9:4 says, "We must work the works of him who sent me while it is day; night comes, when no one can work."

SPECIFIC IDEAS FOR STEWARDS OF LIFE

As a reminder of our potential and possibilities, here is a list of specific challenges for stewards of life. It is suggestive, not exhaustive. Some items, such as praying, are meant for us all; others may be appropriate only for some.

1. Pray.

Our weakness before the powerful institutions of death drive us to "pray continually."[1] In prayer, we confess our own sins and not just the sins of others. We repent of our arrogance, pride, and greed. We give thanks for the mercy and promises of God. We intercede on behalf of all, including our enemies. In prayer, we ask to be enabled to do by God's power what we are unable to do on our own.

2. Study the Bible.

Start with the Gospels, and then read the rest of the New Testament. Focus on what is revealed about Jesus and by Jesus. Note that Jesus is a staunch defender of people and of life. Then study the Old Testament through the lens of Christ and the great prophets. Let the scriptures be a witness to the God of life and love.

3. Study the witness of prophetic voices.

The most helpful Christian thinkers are those who combine an evangelical (in the historic sense of the word, meaning having an understanding of the gospel) perspective with a deep commitment to justice, peace, and fullness of life for all of God's children. Leo Tolstoy's *The Kingdom of God and Peace Essays* and the writings of Mahatma Gandhi and Martin Luther King, Jr., are modern classics. *Nuclear Holocaust and Christian Hope* by Ronald Sider and Richard Taylor abounds in significant insights for Christian peacemakers. *Sojourners* magazine speaks from an evangelical perspective on issues of peace and justice.

4. *Study the state of the world.*

Karl Barth once said, "Take your Bible and take your newspaper, and read both. But interpret newspapers from your Bible."[2] Read *The Game of Disarmament* by Alva Myrdal, who received the Nobel Prize, and Alan Geyer's *The Idea of Disarmament.* Study Lester Brown's *Building a Sustainable Society* and other writings. Learn how the arms race is robbing resources from the essential work of creating regenerative agriculture and sustainable ecological systems.

5. *Study and discuss together.*

Invite others to join in study and conversation. Plan Bible studies on alternatives to violence as revealed in the life and teachings of Jesus. Start a book club. When texts talk about stewardship of life, discuss the issues of life and death not from the perspective of a political party but from the perspective of the scriptures. Hold adult and youth forums focusing on abortion, war, mercy killing, and the death penalty.

6. *Learn from the scientific and intellectual community.*

Read the *Bulletin of the Atomic Scientists* and become familiar with the Union of Concerned Scientists and groups like SANE (the Committee for a Sane Nuclear Policy) and the Council for a Livable World. Read *Indefensible Weapons* by Robert Lifton and Richard Falk. Information from these sources will enable you to say no to arms escalation and say yes to realistic alternatives to the militarization of the world.

7. *Learn from enlightened military leaders.*

Support the work of the Center for Defense Information in Washington, DC, which supports a strong defense but opposes policies that increase the danger of nuclear war. Remind all who still believe in military solutions to human problems of this statement from General Douglas MacArthur: "In the evolution of civilization, if it is to survive, all men cannot fail eventually to adopt Gandhi's belief that the process of mass applications of force to resolve contentious issues is fundamentally not only wrong but contains within itself the germs of self-destruction."[3]

8. *Practice peacemaking in your personal relationships.*

Read *Getting to Yes* by Roger Fisher and William Ury. Learn commonsense methods of resolving personal conflicts peacefully. Think of how these principles can prevent violence in community and global conflicts.

9. *Write and speak for life.*

Share your convictions in letters to elected representatives and your local newspaper. Write often; express appreciation as well as criticism. Invite friends and neighbors to your home for discussion of these issues. Speak out on these themes at your service or professional club or women's circle. If you are not a public speaker, have a video or film presentation.

10. *Participate in the political process.*

Vote! We should work for life through the political process, beginning with local offices and measures. Both parties, Republicans and Democrats, need to be challenged to affirm life and deny the institutions of death. Participate in rallies and marches for life to dramatize the depth of your convictions.

11. Examine your vocational commitment.

Does your daily work support an institution of death? All who work in such fields must come to terms with their own consciences in this regard; none should carelessly avoid the issue. If we are working to prepare for unjustifiable warfare, there may be no alternative but to refuse to support it by our labor.

12. Consider conscientious objection.

The moral issues of military service should be discussed in Sunday school, confirmation, and young-adult groups long before the day of induction. We should not tell young people *what to think*, but we should help them *to think* so that they will not drift thoughtlessly, through peer pressure or jingoistic propaganda, into military service. Some taxpaying adults opposed to war making have refused payment of the portion of their taxes earmarked for military purposes or doomsday weapons. Others have paid their taxes in full while enclosing a letter of protest.

13. Support a national peace academy.

We spend billions on basic military training and the national military academies and war colleges but next to nothing on learning the arts of peacemaking. Proposals calling for the establishment of a national academy of peace and conflict resolution are regularly introduced in Congress; urge your senators and representatives to back these efforts. If the day is ever to come when "nation shall not lift up sword against nation, neither shall they learn war anymore,"[4] we must not only stop learning war but start learning peace.

14. *Become an advocate of civilian-based, nonviolent defense.*

Ponder the possibilities and problems of defeating aggressors and overcoming oppressors by nonviolent noncooperation. Urge our political leaders to follow Sweden's example in designating a portion of the military budget for the study of and training in civilian-based defense.

15. *If it fits you, support and join life-affirming groups.*

Give your support to groups such as the National Coalition to Abolish the Death Penalty, Amnesty International, Prolifers for Survival, Feminists for Life, and Evangelicals for Social Action that promote life, peace, equality, and justice. If you are a medical doctor, nurse, or healthcare provider, join Physicians for Social Responsibility. If an educator, join Engaging Schools. Women, join Women against Military Madness. Similar groups exist for lawyers, scientists, and other professionals. If none fit you, consider starting your own group.

16. *Work to strengthen and reform the United Nations.*

Become familiar with proposals to reform the UN and give it authority appropriate to its responsibility. The UN is an essential but flawed organization; without it, the world would be a more dangerous place. Those who complain of what it costs us to belong to the UN should be reminded that because its headquarters is in New York City, the UN's contribution to the economy of New York more than makes up for its cost.

17. Visit the homelands of our "enemies."

Take a trip to Russia. Visit places such as Central America, the Middle East, and China. Encourage massive educational, economic, and cultural exchanges between countries whose governments are at enmity with each other. Discover for yourself, and encourage others to discover, that there are human beings who yearn for peace, freedom, and justice in every country on earth.

18. Learn from and support the peace churches and caring agencies.

Become acquainted with the Quakers, the Mennonites, and the Church of the Brethren. Support the work of the American Friends Service Committee and the Fellowship of Reconciliation. Read *Fellowship* magazine. Learn about militant nonviolence. Contribute to agencies for global development and food assistance. Support organizations like Bread for the World that work for justice, peace, and fullness of life for all people.

19. Teach your children reverence for life and peace.

G.I. Joe and other war toys that teach violence and irreverence for life are inappropriate gifts for children. When we celebrate the birth of the "Prince of Peace"[5] and "Author of life,"[6] teach your children that those who lack the strength and intelligence to solve conflicts by nonviolent means are weak and foolish. Teach them that Jesus is strong and that people like Hitler are sick and sinful in their attitudes and actions. Tell your children about Gandhi, Martin Luther King, Jr., Albert Schweitzer, Albert Einstein, and others who had the wisdom and strength to renounce violence and affirm the intelligent resolution of human conflict.

20. Remember—we've only just begun.

When it seems that humanity has failed to create a just society with peace and fullness of life for all God's children, remember our youthfulness. Humanity is still in its childhood, or at least not beyond its adolescence. We've only just begun to solve the problems of living together. We are tempted to disparage the dinosaurs who were "too dumb" to survive, but we had best not be too proud. There is evidence that dinosaurs dominated life on this planet for seventy-five million years! If humanity is to survive for the next thousand years (let alone seventy-five million), we must destroy the old institutions of death and create new institutions of life.

SUMMING UP

In *The Politics of Jesus,* John Howard Yoder points to our idolatrous dependence on material goods and our use of violence as two of the most glaring examples of our disharmony with the way of Jesus. The two are closely related. Having too much to defend, we become excessively preoccupied with preserving it, even with violent means. Similarly, in defending our rights, we often ignore and even deny the rights of others, especially those of the weakest among us.

Most Christians today live in conformity with the violent world, contrary to the teachings of the Prince of Peace. The challenges of the present crisis and the voice of Jesus unite in calling us to repent and turn from the old ways of death to new ways of life. We are called to replace oppression with justice, accusation with reconciliation, tribalism with globalism, vengeance with rehabilitation, killing with caring, the sword with the cross, and, above all, death with life. The voice of the living and life-giving Christ joins with the voices of all God's children to exhort us to work for peace and life in all we do.

Coming Out Queer, Coming Out Christian

≡ Brenda Bos ≡

I AM A QUEER[1] pastor. I love Jesus. I love my wife. Both these loves make me scandalous.

I am ordained in the Evangelical Lutheran Church in America (ELCA), a denomination that began openly ordaining lesbian and gay pastors in 2009. Like most mainline denominations, the ELCA struggled with this decision. The church acknowledged the gifts of LGBTQIA+[2] pastors and seminarians, and after much prayer and debate, decided to allow qualified queer candidates to be ordained. The day this decision was made, half of the denomination lamented their church was no longer a place they knew, and the other half finally felt their church's theology and policies matched their own sense of God's call.

Of course, this decision could only be made because faithful pastors and seminarians decided to come out and express their whole selves to God and to their church. Those who came out followed a long line of brave members of the LGBTQIA+ community.

At the beginning of the HIV/AIDS crisis, a group of six gay activists in New York City plastered the city with posters featuring the slogan "Silence=Death" and a pink triangle on a black background. The Silence=Death Project, as these activists came to be known, "drew parallels between the Nazi period and the AIDS crisis, declaring that 'silence about the oppression and annihilation of gay people, then and now, must be broken as a matter of our survival.' The slogan thus protested both taboos around discussion of safer sex and the unwillingness of some to resist societal injustice and governmental indifference."[3] The pink triangle was worn by homosexuals in Nazi concentration camps and relegated wearers to the absolute bottom of the camp social system. The pink triangle was also reclaimed as a sign of solidarity instead of humiliation by ACT UP, or the AIDS Coalition to Unleash Power, an advocacy group formed in 1987 to call for legislation and medical research to combat AIDS.

HIV/AIDS patients and their lovers, families, and friends were silenced out of shame. Whispers abounded that HIV/AIDS was God's way of punishing sinners. Of course, this belief was proved false once the epidemic spread to women, hemophiliacs, and children. AIDS was and is a human disease, contracted by everyday people living everyday lives, not a divine curse against the wicked.

Still, a diagnosis of HIV/AIDS or "gay cancer" brought incredible shame to families. Infected men could not share their diagnosis with loved ones. Indeed, many men only came out to their families on their death beds or were outed at their funerals when the cause of death was revealed. The spiritual and emotional agony of this silence can never be overstated.

In the LGBTQIA+ community, silence is still not an option. Lesbian, gay, and bisexual teens attempt suicide almost five times more frequently than heterosexual youth,[4] with between 23 percent of lesbian, gay, and bisexual youth attempting to end their lives.[5] LGBTQIA+ youth represent about 14 percent of the youth population,[6] but the Williams Institute at UCLA Law School reports LGBTQIA+ youth make up 40 percent of the youth homeless population.[7] LGBTQIA+ youth end up on the street mostly because of family rejection or family abuse. Many LGBTQIA+ youth are too afraid of rejection and violence to come out. Staying in the closet is profoundly damaging to souls and bodies.

And so, members of the LGBTQIA+ community *must* come out, boldly and with great joy, whatever their situation in life. San Francisco supervisor Harvey Milk first called for a mass coming out in the mid-1970s. Milk knew the only way the queer community would ever be publicly recognized, accepted, and even celebrated was by letting people know the gays were not some strange group of miscreants hiding in back alleys. The gays were their family members, their storeowners, their teachers, the kid next door, the football coach, or those nice old people who live down the street. The gays were their *clergy*.

As sexual abuse scandals continue to emerge in the Roman Catholic and other churches, some of us hold our breath when we talk about gay clergypeople. We fear the specter of sexual abuse of minors is always lurking.

This is exactly why LGBTQIA+ people need to come out—to demonstrate that not all, or even most, LGBTQIA+ people are sexual deviants, let alone sexual predators. To come out is to show that most LGBTQIA+ people seek mutually affirming, consensual relationships.

Rev. Elizabeth Edman celebrates the parallels between coming out as LGBTQIA+ and coming out as a Christian in *Queer Virtue: What LGBTQ People Know about Life and Love and How It Can Revitalize Christianity.*[8] She notes that coming out as queer requires a deep sense of self, as does coming out as Christian. To reveal oneself as queer requires courage and a stronger desire to be known than to remain safely closeted. The same *should* be true of revealing ourselves as Christians, but many of us fear we would be alienated if we told our friends we love Jesus.

Queer virtue asks that we touch people, physically and spiritually. Many people who distrust the queer community think queer physical touch is perverse, unwanted, and cruel. This is not true, but most homophobic people, if they are honest, say imagining "perverse" sexual activity is what disturbs them the most. However, when they realize spiritual connection between two people is a critical component of queer life, they may be forced to reconsider their assumptions.

Queer spirituality can be vibrant, diverse, undefinable, and staggeringly beautiful. Queer spirituality may be celebrated in traditional religious settings, like a church or a mosque, or in alternative venues. Since many queer folks were rejected by religious authorities or traditionally pious families, they may never feel safe in classic ecclesial settings.

Queer spirituality is defined by its courage, its mutuality, and its desire for justice. When LGBTQIA+ people realize they are made in God's image, they see a God who is diverse, unique, loves in a variety of ways, and expresses the divine self *queerly*. Queerness is not merely a sexual or gender expression but also a diverse, undefinable, expansive form of self-expression. A person who comes out queer achieves a wholeness that causes the soul to sing. This spirituality is a gift to the wider community.

Living in the closet or experiencing profound rejection inflicts deep spiritual wounds. Consider suicidal LGBTQIA+ teens who have just been kicked out of their homes. On top of everything else, they are also having a *spiritual crisis*. I do not mean to say they need to reconcile with God; I mean to say their soul has been crushed by the human rejection they are experiencing. Homelessness and suicidal thoughts are *spiritual crises* as well as mental and physical crises.

Therefore, to come out as queer in our communities is to provide spiritual healing. As fully integrated, healthy, spiritually vibrant LGBTQIA+ people come out, others will see this way of living is possible. Those of us who are mired in shame and guilt because of who we were told we are (disgusting, sinners, dirty, and not "real men," not to mention all the derogatory slang words used against the LGBTQIA+ community) may get the chance to find healing and wholeness. Could it be that God loves us? Could it be that this strange queer identity we have is a gift from God?

This is Christian love, pure and simple. This is healing and hope for LGBTQIA+ people who never dared to dream they were loved. It also provides healing and hope for the wider community, which begins to see God's love and God's gifts in fresh new ways. As we come out as queer or Christian, we become a lighthouse shining a beacon to guide those who struggle in a stormy sea.

Silence is not an option in the LGBTQIA+ community. But it is also not an option in communities of faith. Who cares if we have a relationship with our Creator *if we do not have a relationship with the created*? In times of turmoil and confusion, people of faith *must* come out as compassionate, forgiving, curious people. We *must* build communities in places of brokenness. We *must* be courageous with our whole persons and all our love. God has created us to love diversely and deeply, even at great personal risk. The queer community is uniquely qualified to teach us and to lead us in this mission.

Preaching Grace

⇒ Christine M. Smith ⇐

WHEN I CONTEMPLATE WHAT transforming message of hope might be spoken and embodied in the face of heterosexist condemnation, I always return to grace. The grace of God becomes one of the most powerful messages preachers and religious communities might proclaim in faithful response to the violence of heterosexism and homophobia. The grace of God and the grace-filled love of human beings are powerful forces in human history. This power can shatter prisons of gender domination and submission, expose illusions of moral and ethical superiority, transform judgments into moments of profound acceptance, and empower us to dwell in the realm of mystery rather than condemnation.

The essence of this grace is God, but human beings within Christian communities are called also to become agents of grace-filled action and speech in the world. Susan Brooks Thistlethwaite and Mary Potter Engel clearly acknowledge the importance and power of grace in North American black, feminist, Native American, and gay and lesbian liberation theologies. They say, "Grace as the divine empowering of human beings (and of all creaturely and natural life) to live and work for a just and loving world has traditionally been spoken of as sanctification, the process of being made and making holy/whole."[1] God's distinctive love and grace are central to the task, but human agency in the work of reconciliation, community building, and justice making is central to a liberationist perspective on grace. In liberation theology, grace has less to do with the forgiveness of individual sins, and more to do with confronting and transforming social and systemic forces and structures that produce evil. In describing the voices of many liberation theologians, Engel and Thistlethwaite say, "They speak of grace as the divine empowering that heals the external and internal wounds inflicted on individuals and peoples by structures of oppression and as the divine empowering that liberates peoples from the bondage of systemic evil."[2]

Grace empowers human beings to participate in the redemptive processes of transformation and justice. The work of sanctifying grace accepts, empowers, indicts, exposes, and embraces. A grace that renders creation holy and participates in the liberation of all people is a grace that does not know or understand the boundaries of human acceptance. It is a love that empowers those whom society would strip of power. It is a grace that indicts and exposes all those human realities that destroy sacred community and embodied justice. And it is a love that eternally lifts, embraces, and calls people home. This grace and the work that it inspires are terrifying and exhilarating. This grace makes an enormous and total claim upon each of us and our religious communities.

How might a liberationist perspective on grace enable us to do the kind of sanctifying work that needs to be done in response to heterosexist condemnation? What claims will it make upon us? What truths will it reveal to us? What hope does it engender? In response to these questions and others, I want to look first at the *home* of grace; then I will examine two dimensions of human

agency—dwelling in mystery and salvific deliverance from fear—
that give us a picture of what sanctifying grace might look like in
our day.

THE HOME OF GRACE

Liberation theology begins its task by looking at the concrete experience and reality of oppression. Out of their particular experiences
of condemnation and oppression, lesbians and gay men know a
great deal about exiled existence and being exiled from home. If
the Christian church and other religious communities will see
these men and women as our teachers, we might understand more
fully the nature of grace.

John Fortunato, reflecting on the spiritual journey of gay
Christians, describes a profound existential truth about many
of their lives when he says, "When you put all of the particulars
together, the gestalt is oppression. The experience is not of moving
from one particular to another; it is a constant, chronic feeling
of not belonging, of being threatened and rejected."[3] Perhaps all
human beings can identify with the personal experience of feeling
that one does not belong, or that one is threatened or rejected. The
major difference is that our society *intends* and *structures* this reality
for lesbians and gay men. If grace is a divine empowering toward
human wholeness, toward shalom, and toward the just structur-
ing of human relations, then this aggressive condemnation is the
antithesis of grace. In deepest contrast to experiences of rejection
and threat, the work of grace creates acceptance and an environment of safety. It is impossible to be engaged simultaneously in the
work of condemnation and the work of grace.

In a provocative article about the way God ushers in a new
economy, or a new household for the human community, Douglas

Meeks uses the metaphor of home to describe justice. He believes that the experience of home is a basic individual and collective human need. He says

> We have all had, at least fleetingly, an experience of home. Home is where no one ever forgets your name. Home is where no matter what you have done, you will be confronted, forgiven, and accepted. Home is where there is always a place for you at the table and where you can be certain that what is on the table will be shared. To be a part of a home or a household is to have access to life. The heart of justice is participation in God's economy or God's household. Unless the power of God's love creates a household, justice will disintegrate into meaninglessness.[4]

Heterosexism and homophobia keep the Christian community from creating a household in which every created person has a name, shares in the abundance of creation, and is held accountable for the resources and actions of her or his life. The violent fear and condemnation at the center of a heterosexist society and church are attempts to deny all gay men and lesbians access to life. The condemnation and privileges of heterosexism suggest that there is only room at the table for those who are heterosexual. This is the antithesis of sanctifying grace; through sanctifying grace, the sacred nature of all humanity is recognized and named, and resources are distributed in such a way that all might have life.

Christian persons need to understand the power and limitations of our attitudes and actions. Our condemnation may keep many of our religious communities from being *home* for gay and lesbian people, but it will never prevent the essence of God from being the home of grace for all. And let us be clear that when a home is divided by the condemnation of some, it ceases to be a true home for any.

The home of grace has to do with naming and blessing, knowing and embracing. In the last few lines of Marsie Silvestro's "Blessing Song," there is a challenge to the church:

And we'll bless you, our sister
Bless you in our way
And we'll welcome home . . . all the life you've known
And softly speak your name
Oh we'll welcome home all the self you own
And softly speak your name.[5]

The home of grace welcomes *all* the life people have known, all the self people own, and speaks the name of each created one. It is not a blessing free of confrontation or accountability, but it is an embrace of gracious acceptance. It is not a blessing that is free from expectation and work, but it is the assurance of sustaining love.

Chris Glaser speaks about the work of the church as consisting of a people opening up the household of God to others and to all creation. He believes that when the church discerns its true vocation as a kind of threshold for God's love, it will understand that it is the body of Christ standing in a doorway beckoning others to come home.[6] This is the vision of the home of grace. What is the human work that needs to be done in order to create and sustain it?

Standing Your Ground

≡ Paul Tellström ≡

YOU ARE IMPORTANT AND needed. You are important to your neighbors in the forging and keeping of faith and friendships, and you are needed by the community you serve. You have a purpose.

I want to tell you a personal story. I wanted to be a minister since I was eleven years old. Dr. Gambell, my childhood minister, was a greatly respected figure in my community, and he was always kind to me. When he was killed in a car crash and I saw the hole his absence created in the community, I resolved to follow in his footsteps. Later, I realized I was gay, and I left that dream behind when I understood that the Christian church did not want me.

Because good straight allies worked to change things, I eventually attended seminary. I became a leader at the First Congregational Church of Los Angeles, then I interned and attained a minor staff position.

Then came my Ecclesiastical Council, where churches from all over came to meet me, ask questions, and vote on whether I should be ordained. The progressives thought I was a shoo-in and didn't come. Only two churches in the area got the word out that a gay man was going to be ordained and came out to vote.

After a lengthy inquisition and an even more lengthy discussion behind closed doors, I was called back before the Council and told that I would not be endorsed for ordination. I asked why, and the moderator gave a reason that didn't make sense. She was embarrassed. I asked again, and she told me it was my "lifestyle."

Members of my congregation present were appalled. I found my voice that day. In the pulpit, I asked my partner, Carl, to stand, and I introduced him. Carl said, "I'm not going to stand, I'm going to come up there so that you can all see who we are."

I said, "I *will* be ordained." Since I didn't have the power to make that decision, my senior pastor stood up and announced that my church would ordain me independently.

But that wasn't the end of the matter. I was handed a note at my ordination service that said I was subverting the will of Jesus Christ by putting forth my own homosexual agenda, which I didn't even know I could do.

I am the only pastor I know of in my Conference who didn't pass his Ecclesiastical Council. Yet somehow, I was called to the best church in the Conference. And I do mean that. I am so proud of my church.

I understand how it feels to be marginalized and not accepted, especially in a place that is supposed to be a sanctuary where people learn that God loves them; this experience has colored my entire ministry. And I know that many others have similar experiences.

This is why you matter. This is why you are important.

Luke 2:41–52 tells how a twelve-year-old Jesus got separated from his parents in Jerusalem when they headed home but he stayed behind to learn at the temple. Jesus remaining in the temple and scaring Mary and Joseph was disobedient—but ultimately constructive.

The story of Jesus in the temple as a boy offers many lessons. A colleague in Cleveland named Shawnthea Monroe advised me pastor to pastor that we should be where God wants us to be even if it doesn't make sense at the time. We are called into ministry—and we are also called out.

Shawnthea says, "This story about Jesus only made sense later, and not at the time when he wandered away from his parents. Most of life is like that: you live it forward and understand it backward—and God's handiwork is usually obvious but only in hindsight."

What would it look like if the church was constructively disobedient? Would it oppose a culture that demonizes LGBT people, immigrants, and Muslims? A culture that allows homelessness, the destruction of the environment, children going to bed hungry, and people being incarcerated because they fled violence like Joseph, Mary, and Jesus did?

We have already achieved some positive changes—overturning Proposition 8, blessing the Koran when someone threatened to burn one, and taking on the Irvine, California, City Council when they gratuitously removed the living wage ordinance. We walked in marches, attended vigils, allied with like-minded groups working for justice, and provided learning and service opportunities for young people. We've endured uncertainty and upheaval, times when no one was sure of what comes next, and everything worked out in the end. "Risk something big for something good," as William Sloane Coffin once said.[1]

I have baptized many kids and watched them grow into startlingly smart young adults with a healthy worldview and a love of faith and community. *And this is the message in Luke*: our children are ours but only for a time. Joseph and Mary were terrified and probably troubled by Jesus's increasing independence. He was growing beyond them, like all children do.

The same is true for pastors and congregations. Pastors lead and nurture their flock until the congregation either grows beyond its current pastor and *needs* the next one, or the pastor him- or herself must move on.

Leaving is hard but necessary for growth. When the student is ready, the teacher will appear, according to a proverb commonly attributed to the Buddhists.

You are important and needed. *You have a purpose.* You are in exactly the right church in exactly the right place at exactly the right time. You need to know it and believe it. You will bear exactly the right fruit with every stand you take and every statement you make. As Paul said in his letter to the Romans, "If God is for us, who can be against us?"[2]

New Wineskins, New Dimensions

= Larry Rasmussen =

HEAR WELL WHAT RABBI Jesus says:

No one tears a piece from a new garment and sews it on an old garment; otherwise the new will be torn, and the piece from the new will not match the old. And no one puts new wine into old wineskins; otherwise the new wine will burst the skins and will be spilled, and the skins will be destroyed. But new wine must be put into fresh wineskins. And no one after drinking old wine desires new wine, but says, "The old is good."[1]

Jesus said no one does this, but someone must have tried it. Otherwise, Jesus had no reason to instruct his disciples about it. Or maybe he did so because the disciples themselves weren't ready to follow the Way. Maybe they said, "But Rabbi, the old is good. You know that aged wine is better. And our old clothes are good friends."

But what is the new wine and cloth to which *we* must now testify? And why do we say, "Thanks but no thanks, the old is good"?

Have you not seen? Have you not heard? Did you miss it? The planet you were born on, came to love, and grew accustomed to is no longer the planet on which you live. The climatic sweet spot in which all human civilizations have flourished for twelve thousand years is in jeopardy at our hands. Geologists call that sweet spot the Holocene. This epoch was characterized by sufficient climate stability to allow the triumph of life over and again. But the Holocene appears to be segueing into a new epoch, which some are calling the Anthropocene (derived from the Greek word for "human," *anthropos*) because it is characterized by the impact of cumulative human activities on the planet. Even places far from human habitation feel our impact—the polar regions, the oceans, and the air high above our heads. This new age is characterized by climate instability, widespread uncertainty, and mass extinction. Beloved Earth is now a different planet, and the only geological epoch we have ever known is ending. Yet the uncertain ways of a destabilized planet strike us as "rumors of unfathomable things, and because we [cannot] fathom them we [fail] to believe them."[2] Instead we say, "The old wine is good, and so are the trusty old wineskins."

We did not expect the new wine of a new geological age. Who would have thought we could not count on the third rock from the sun the way we always have? Who would have thought our home planet could not be relied on for steady seasons of planting and harvest; for glacial waters feeding great rivers; for sea levels constant enough to host most of the great cities and much of the human population; for sufficient time to let flora and fauna adapt to new insects, predators, and diseases; for rainfall and snowpack and enough resources to ensure that future generations will not only survive but thrive; and for ocean biochemistry stable enough to sustain the underwater rainforests they have sheltered for eons?

How, then, do we compose a new song for a strange land, even though it be our own? It is so much easier to do what Jesus feared we would—namely, do everything we can to put the *new* wine in the *old* wineskins. We try to solve our problems with the same mindset and habits that produced them. We work furiously to get the same fossil-fueled economy and the same gender, sexual, racial, and economic strata back on track, the same systems that will bring more climate change and storms of every kind.

Don't be surprised by this. Elizabeth Kolbert tells the story of Thomas Kuhn, the science historian who gave us the term *paradigm shift*. Kuhn came across a 1949 study by Harvard psychologists about how people process disruptive information entitled "On the Perception of Incongruity: A Paradigm."[3] The Harvard psychologists asked students to identify playing cards shown in quick succession. Easy enough—except that a few had been doctored. The cards included anomalies such as a red six of spades and a black four of hearts. The students struggled to make sense of what they were seeing. Some thought the red spade was actually purple or rusty black. Others thought the symbols were reversed. Some complained that they couldn't make out the suit or that they weren't sure what a spade looked like anymore. Kuhn looked at challenges to scientific theories in light of this deep-seated impulse to force anomalies into familiar frameworks—in other words, to force new wine into old wineskins. Finally, despite the novel information and mounting frustration, someone had the nerve to call a spade a spade—a *red* spade a *red* spade.[4] Then the unfathomable became fathomable as crisis led to insight, and old frameworks and habits gave way to new ones. Paradigms shifted.

Jesus's disciples struggled to make sense of new information too. They knew that Jesus had a startling proclivity for challenging commonsense assumptions. He did it again and again: "Have you never read in the scriptures," he said, "'The stone that the builders rejected has become the cornerstone . . .'?'"[5] He crossed every barrier the disciples deemed insurmountable and reached out to Samaritans, Gentiles, women, children, lepers, the diseased and the disfigured, and outcasts. And what did the disciples do? They tried to protect him from himself and stop him from embracing the pariahs. The time for new wineskins had come, but they held fast to aged wine and comfy clothes. So when Peter was asked three times if he knew Jesus, and he replied, "I do not know this man," he wasn't exactly lying. He didn't know Jesus. The Messiah he *knew* wouldn't end, like so many other Jews, in shame on the Roman cross. Nor was Peter alone. Even after the women reported their amazement at finding Jesus's tomb empty, the disciples on the road to Emmaus said, "We had hoped that he was the one to redeem Israel."[6] But alas, that hope was dashed.

The disciples experienced three shocks. The first and worst was that Rabbi Jesus was cruelly and shamefully put to death and was not the Messiah they left their nets for and dedicated their lives to. But it was also a shock that, in the power of the Holy Spirit, he was still with them, a real, living presence. The tomb was empty. The God who freed enslaved people from Egypt and led exiles home from Babylon was, through Jesus and the Holy Spirit, disrupting the status quo again. The third shock was perhaps the most startling. These followers, those who didn't know Jesus, *were themselves now new wineskins* and full of chutzpah in a new world. The kingdom of God come among *them*, the plain, the common, the wretched of the earth. Their entire *world*, not just a paradigm or two, had shifted. Now they themselves plotted the resurrection.

So buck up, friends. Yes, we face an imminent apocalypse. But even a *scientifically validated* apocalypse is not enough to motivate people to make new wineskins. Evidently, no one who's *scared to death* is going to turn to renewable energy, physical or spiritual, in this tough new age; no one anxious about tomorrow is going to do the right thing with new wine. Howard Thurman was right: "Don't ask what the world needs. Ask what makes you come alive, and go do it."[7]

No, we will not survive the Anthropocene except by faith—faith as the conviction of things not yet seen.[8] But we can have courage, settle in for the long haul, do good works, and hone our skills in tanning new wineskins.

Take your cue from Katharine White, writer and editor for the *New Yorker*. After she died, her husband, E. B. White, collected her essays for a book on gardening. He wrote an introduction that ends with a description of Katharine in the fall, planning the spring garden she knew she would not see:

Armed with a diagram and a clipboard, Katharine would get into a shabby old Brooks raincoat much too long for her, put on a little round wool hat, pull on a pair of over-shoes, and proceed to the director's chair—a folding canvas thing—that had been placed for her at the edge of the plot. There she would sit, hour after hour, in the wind and the weather, while Henry Allen produced dozens of brown paper packages of new bulbs and a basketful of old ones, ready for the intricate interment. As the years went by and age overtook her, there was something comical yet touching in her bedraggled appearance on this awesome occasion—the small, hunched-over figure, her studied absorption in the implausible notion that there would yet be another spring, oblivious to the ending of her own days, which she knew perfectly well was near at hand, sitting there with her detailed chart under those dark skies in the dying October, calmly plotting the resurrection.[9]

There you have your vocation, plain and clear: to put on your boots, pick up your clipboard, lose yourself in wonder, and calmly plot the resurrection. It's time for new wineskins.

The Scandal of Voter Suppression

⇒ Jim Wallis ⇐

IN 2016, VOTERS FACED extensive efforts to make voting more difficult, particularly for people of color and those who are poor. These efforts at voter suppression occurred as a result of GOP gains in governors' races and state legislatures while Barack Obama was president—and also as a result of the Supreme Court gutting a key provision of the Voting Rights Act in 2013.

Between those two factors, 23 states—including some key battlegrounds in the presidential election—had new voter restrictions in place for the 2016 election. Examples include laws that eliminated polling places or moved them to less accessible locations, reduced polling hours, tightened voter-ID requirements, "purged" voter rolls, and reduced early voting and Sunday voting, which are popular among minority voters in certain regions.

As we approach the 2018 midterms, we need to protect the right to vote for citizens of all races, economic levels, and political persuasions. This is an *imago dei* issue: If we believe that all human beings are created in the image of God (Genesis 1:26), then efforts to prevent some of God's children from exercising their franchise must be opposed as a matter of fidelity to our faith. It's also a Matthew 25 issue: If we believe that how we treat people living in poverty and those who have been caught up in the system of mass incarceration is how we treat Christ himself, then we have a clear Christian mandate to ensure that society's most vulnerable can exercise the right to vote.

In-person voter fraud is vanishingly rare, to the tune of only 31 documented cases out of *1 billion* ballots cast between 2000 and 2014. To put it another way, the odds that any given person will attempt in-person voter fraud are something like 1 in 32 million, significantly lower than the odds of being struck by lightning. Twice.

Stricter ID requirements and other measures claimed to combat "voter fraud" are actually efforts to suppress the vote of certain people. As Christians living in a representative democracy, we should champion the right of all people to participate in the act of self-government by exercising their right to vote, regardless of who they vote for.

Because protecting voters is integral to creating the just society our faith calls us to seek, *Sojourners* has long worked with other faith groups, such as the National African American Clergy Network, as well as groups of legal professionals, such as the Lawyers' Committee for Civil Rights Under Law, to bring lawyers and clergy together for discussion and action centered on protecting vulnerable voters. This year, we are expanding our involvement in this area through a new "Lawyers and Collars" initiative that will involve lawyers and clergy working together in important and innovative ways.

There is symbolic power in clergy, wearing their clerical collars, showing up alongside lawyers on Election Day to offer protection to voters who may be targeted for suppression or intimidation, and that work will continue and expand this November at polling places across the country.

However, there is also much that can be done—and needs to be done—well before Election Day. For example, in 24 states the chief election official is an elected secretary of state. The secretary of state has broad powers over how elections are administered and can make it easier or more difficult for voters to exercise their franchise. Because these are mostly elected officials, they must respond to public pressure from constituents if they want to keep their jobs—which is why we plan to have lawyers and clergy in a number of states work with the secretary of state's office to ensure voters are protected, and in some cases let officials know that we're watching them.

Another way we can stand for vulnerable people is to vote ourselves—in elections at every level of government and on ballot initiatives. This fall, for example, an initiative on the ballot in Florida would return the right to vote to more than a million people with felony convictions, many of whom committed relatively minor, nonviolent drug crimes, and all of whom have paid their debt to society. Several states have passed measures to make it easier to register to vote, and others have introduced legislation to do so that so far lacks sufficient support. Electing state legislators, governors, and secretaries of state who support voting rights is something we all can do by exercising our own right to vote.

In a representative democracy, the right to vote is one of the most fundamental a person can have, and a prerequisite for retaining a host of other rights and protections. We must protect this most basic of rights for all our brothers and sisters, and that work must start well before any ballots are cast.

The Teachings of the Reverend
Dr. James M. Lawson, Jr.

⇒ Ashley Herndon ⇐

OVER TWO YEARS AGO, a friend, the Reverend Ken Wyant, introduced me to the Reverend Dr. James M. Lawson's workshops and the impact of his work in practicing and teaching nonviolence. Now I would rather take a poke in the eye with a sharp stick than miss a session. I cannot say that as a young man I was nonviolent in all things, but my family and church tried. Dr. Lawson has pulled it off. Here, I will try to briefly summarize his teachings.

Dr. Lawson's ideas revolve around revolutions—in particular, (1) the American Revolution, (2) Mahatma Gandhi's Salt March to the Sea, (3) the period of change in the 1940s–1970s in the United States, and (4) today's activism in this country.

The first revolution gave us two preambles that power the third and fourth:

- Declaration of Independence: "We hold these truths to be self-evident, that all men are created equal, that they are endowed by their Creator with certain unalienable Rights, that among these are Life, Liberty, and the pursuit of Happiness."

- Constitution of the United States: "We the People of the United States, in Order to form a more perfect Union, establish Justice, insure domestic Tranquility, provide for the common defence, promote the general Welfare, and secure the Blessings of Liberty to ourselves and our Posterity, do ordain and establish this Constitution for the United States of America."

Today, good people are being manipulated by long-held fears and evolutionary tribalistic conflict. One side accuses the other of not following the Founding Fathers' constructs. I wish I knew what those were, especially since some of the founders were slave owners and money changers. But these men assembled a group of words that had never before been put together in such a manner, as seen above. However, we must realize that it did not take long to add ten amendments known as the Bill of Rights.

Plantation capitalism was alive and practiced in all the colonies, then in the states, supplanted by "gangster capitalism," which is prevalent in our current society. The idea of neighbor and neighborhood is lacking, and folks are protesting about a geometrically growing number of complaints. The concept and sense of community have ebbed accordingly.

The single idea of human rights and agape has been slowly disappearing—again. Consider these questions (along with Dr. Lawson's answers):

- Who is our neighbor today? (We are.)
- How is my neighbor impacted by plantation capitalism turned gangster capitalism? (There is an ephemeral and lasting loss of community that splits us and defeats us.)

- What force silences us? (It's the fear of embarrassment.)
- Why is love of neighbor central to Jesus's teaching? (It makes the world go around.)
- How can we break the silence on behalf of our neighbors? (We can listen without judgment and not be complicit by remaining silent.)

The year 1876 marks the destruction of Reconstruction. However, the power structure referred to as the plantation capitalists persisted, including large and corporate farms and major industries, controlling wages, and ensuring unequal opportunity.

However, we have a tool that cannot be defeated: nonviolence. Nonviolence is the science of social change. Gandhi fathered nonviolence just as Einstein fathered much of natural science. Nonviolence was designed to be the opposite of racism. Nonviolence is also the opposite of other "isms" that hold the "other" in contempt. Since the US revolution of the last century has begun to be dismantled by the power structure legislatively and judicially, it is again time to resist.

We are taught that you cannot defeat evil with evil nor can you right a wrong with another wrong. Nonviolence is the proven way. Sadly, this is rarely taught in schools or universities today.

In volume 2 of *The Politics of Nonviolent Action*, Gene Sharp lists 198 methods and tactics of direct action. And now there are even more—but none as powerful as nonviolence, also known as soul force, God force, and agape. Since violence is created by fear, soul force is the defense.

The military successfully uses strategy, patience, and planning, and the resistance must do the same. Change takes time followed by concerted continuous action. Courage and strength—not fists—certainly help.

A LITTLE ABOUT DR. LAWSON

Imagine a ninety-year-old dynamo. That is Dr. Lawson, a teacher, pastor, leader, practitioner, student, and tireless cheerleader for human rights and freedom. He teaches the use of freedom language, value, duty, and country. Value is the life force, duty is action, and country is the community. If we are willing to listen, learn, and work based on what worked for Gandhi, Bonhoeffer, King, and Lawson, we too can experience the joy of Satyagraha (soul force).

Dr. Lawson discusses the hard parts of history, those the power structure does not want or in many cases allow to be taught. He has so much to say, I hope I can succinctly share his major premises.

Dr. Lawson is pastor emeritus of Holman United Methodist Church. He is a patriot and was a coworker and fellow of the Reverend Dr. Martin Luther King, Jr. Dr. Lawson was reared and educated in Ohio, and in 1958 at Oberlin University, he was asked by Dr. King to come to the South and work with the Southern Christian Leadership Conference. "We need you" were some of the persuasive words used. Both men knew that it was not just the South that needed help; other sections of the country were just as unequal and controlled by the power structure. Since both men were scholars of Gandhi's methods, it was a perfect fit.

As an associate and activist, Dr. Lawson was the planner, mover, and leader of the sit-ins that desegregated downtown Nashville, Tennessee. He was active in the movements in Albany, Georgia; Birmingham, Alabama; and St. Augustine, Florida; the Freedom Rides; and many other movements leading up to the sanitation workers' strike in Memphis. He invited Dr. King to speak in Memphis, and Dr. King was assassinated the day after his speech there. Dr. Lawson's experience is nearly unequalled.

I consider the terms *neighbor, neighborhood,* and *community* to be interconnected, with one leading to the other. This chain begins with one-on-one encounters leading to two-on-two, ten-on-ten, and one-hundred-on-one-hundred like minds willing to work together for one purpose: human dignity and freedom. The phrase used by the Memphis strikers is apropos: "I Am a Man," which had nothing to do with gender and everything to do with human dignity.

A neighbor is one, a neighborhood is a geographic place, and community can be anywhere and everywhere there are like believers. The love of people as lived by Dr. Lawson creates change.

President Ronald Reagan paraphrased Matthew 5:14 when he called the USA "the shining city upon the hill." (Jesus used the article *a,* not *the,* but maybe we can become *the* shining city.) I believe it was Governor John Winthrop who added "the eyes of all people are upon us" when addressing the Puritans. These leaders' depiction is still achievable. Ralph McGill, the progressive former editor of the *Atlanta Constitution* who wrote *The Fleas Come with the Dog,* added that in his day, our country was "wearing a new evening gown with a dirty slip showing."[1] That description fits today just as it did in the middle of the twentieth century.

Of course, not all dogs have fleas. But these are some of the fleas Dr. Lawson exposes:

1. Plantation capitalism
2. Racism
3. Sexism
4. Militarism
5. Monetary structuralism
6. Genderism
7. Other "isms"

As Pogo once said, "We have met the enemy and he is us!"

CORE PRINCIPLES OF DR. LAWSON

The link between theory and practice is very close in nonviolent civil resistance, so Dr. Lawson focuses on six core concepts for organizing nonviolent resistance struggles:

1. Power and struggle
2. Recovering nonviolent power
3. Strategy, tactics, and methods in waging nonviolent struggles
4. Challenges and facing fear
5. Language of the newly emerging society
6. Communications, messaging, and slogans

During the 1960s, it was accepted wisdom among organizers that to achieve any lasting change in the United States, one must organize the South. Drs. King and Lawson admonished those who felt the South was the only unequal region. They began their work there, but the movement became national and then global as it moved to other continents. Nonviolence works. They encouraged new ideas but proved that a focus on one goal is paramount, not multiple strikes at different targets.

Unity means one message, many voices. Drs. King and Lawson felt that dispersed activism now and then is not useful because there is no continuity, or at least not enough for an idea to capture attention and create change. They recommended a regional approach of building local communities of like minds, growing from two to many.

They warned that it will not be easy or nonconfrontational. Ask Representative John Lewis and others how it felt to be beaten—harshly. However, *nonviolence* means nonviolence. Never use fists or violent words. Agape can defeat the evil use of power.

Jesus taught that you cannot pick grapes from a briar patch. You must plant seeds from a grapevine, nourish them, grow them, and then harvest the fruit.

Dr. Lawson reminds us we are a romantic bunch of folks. By *romantic,* he means that we believe the next generation will make the necessary changes. But is that a realistic expectation? Not as long as we continue doing what we have done before. Change takes massive pressure from the community of believers. Gandhi taught and Dr. Lawson reminds us that sometimes half-hearted activism is worse than doing nothing. So, the answer is to strategize, plan, recruit, build, work, and persevere with like-minded people working on one goal. But do something, or get out of the way.

Since communities are under siege, the old blueprints of power do not work. Honesty and love are needed to create new power structures and grow a community from the few to hundreds to thousands.

Gandhi's Salt March is the perfect example: it began with a small group of supporters and ended with tens of thousands by the time they reached the coast. It marked the beginning of the end for the British Empire.

In December 1955 in Montgomery, Alabama, a lone black woman refused to give up her seat on a bus. Defiance nonviolently led to a year-long strike that broke the segregation of buses and started the Parks-King movement for freedom and social justice. This twenty-year movement changed the world. Thanks, Rosa Parks.

President Lyndon Johnson said, in essence, "You want change? Make me do it!" So people did: the Civil Rights Act, the Voting Rights Act, the desegregation of schools, the debunking negative thinking about the "others," the repeal of sexist and racist laws, and so on. But in today's world, the autocracy is slowly taking back what it can, sometimes covertly and sometimes overtly. We need to act now!

MERGE THE FOUNDERS' PREAMBLE WORDS WITH SOUL FORCE, NOT HATE AND RAGE

There are eight hundred thousand dreamers here and more on the way. It is time to do ordinary things in an unordinary manner. That is what Dr. Lawson teaches. The good doctor adds, "Do it now," and do it with class.

We each have a bit of the cosmic dust from the big bang in our beings and our souls. Put that creative power to work; it can do anything. Become imbued with the spirit of the movement and do not stop. Get fired up.

A good tool to get you motivated is the little book *Martin Luther King and the Montgomery Story*. Read it; then you too may be ready to walk through hellfire to promote human rights and social justice. That is what we can learn from the Reverend Dr. James M. Lawson, Jr. We too can walk the walk—through love and devotion.

The Shakertown Pledge

SOME YEARS AGO, A group of social justice advocates met for a gathering at a retreat near Shakertown in Pennsylvania. Out of this gathering came this pledge that all the participants signed.

Recognizing that the earth and the fullness thereof is a gift from our God, and that we are called to cherish, nurture, and provide loving stewardship for the earth's resources, and recognizing that life itself is a gift, and a call to responsibility, joy and celebration, I make the following declaration:

- I declare myself to be a world citizen.
- I commit myself to lead an ecologically sound life.
- I commit myself to lead a life of creative simplicity and to share my personal wealth with the world's poor.
- I commit myself to join with others in reshaping institutions in order to bring about a more just global society in which each person has full access to the needed resources for their physical, emotional, intellectual and spiritual growth.

- I commit myself to occupational accountability, and in so doing will seek to avoid the creation of products which cause harm.
- I affirm the gift of my body, and commit myself to its proper nourishment and physical well-being.
- I commit myself to examine continually my relations with others and to attempt to relate honestly, morally and lovingly to those around me.
- I commit myself to personal renewal through prayer, meditation and study.
- I commit myself to responsible participation in a community of faith.

Endnotes

PREFACE

1. Carol Rittner and Sondra Meyers, *The Courage to Care: Rescuers of Jews During the Holocaust* (New York: New York University Press, 1986), 2.
2. John 1:23 (New Revised Standard Version).
3. Matt. 3:2 (NRSV).

I. BREAKING THE SILENCE

Is This a Bonhoeffer Moment?: Thomas K. Johnson

1. Stephen R. Haynes and Lori Brandt Hale, *Bonhoeffer for Armchair Theologians* (Louisville: Westminster John Knox Press, 2009), 29.
2. Dietrich Bonhoeffer, *Letters and Papers from Prison* (New York: Touchstone, 1997), 382.
3. Lori Brandt Hale and Reggie L. Williams, "Is This a Bonhoeffer Moment?: Lessons for American Christians from the Confessing Church in Germany," *Sojourners*, February 2018, https://sojo.net /magazine /february-2018/bonhoeffer- moment.
4. Hale and Williams.
5. Dietrich Bonhoeffer, *I Want to Live These Days with You: A Year of Daily Devotions*, trans. O. C. Dean, Jr. (Louisville: Westminster John Knox Press, 2005), 267.

Preaching: Breaking Silence: Christine M. Smith

1. Susan Brooks Thistlethwaite and Mary Potter Engel, eds., *Lift Every Voice: Constructing Christian Theologies from the Underside* (San Francisco: Harper & Row, 1990), 166.
2. Marie M. Fortune, "Forgiveness: The Last Step," in Anne L. Horton and Judith A. Williamson, eds., *Abuse and Religion: When Praying Isn't Enough* (Lexington, Mass.: Lexington Books, 1988), 217.
3. Mary Potter Engel, "Evil, Sin, and Violation of the Vulnerable," in Thistlethwaite and Engel, *Lift Every Voice*, 156–162. In these pages Engel is constructing a fundamentally new understanding of sin.
4. Engel, 156.

5. Joanne Carlson Brown and Carol R. Bohn, eds., *Christianity, Patriarchy, and Abuse: A Feminist Critique* (New York: Pilgrim Press, 1989), 2.
6. Engel, "Evil, Sin, and Violation," 160.
7. Brown and Bohn, *Christianity, Patriarchy, and Abuse,* 107.
8. Brown and Bohn, 105–115. Bohn critiques the kind of theology of owner-ship that is at the heart of much of Christian theology.
9. Brown and Bohn, 105.
10. Brown and Bohn, 113.
11. Brown and Bohn, 114.
12. Brown and Bohn, 114.
13. Brown and Bohn, 115.
14. Fortune, "Forgiveness," 216.
15. Suggested by "What Does It Take?" in Cherrie Moraga, *Loving in the War Years* (Boston: South End Press, 1983), 65–66.

Why I March: Vivian Elaine Johnson

1. United Nations, *The World's Women 2015: Trends and Statistics* (New York: United Nations, 2015), 79, https://unstats.un.org/unsd/gender/downloads/worldswomen2015_report.pdf.
2. United Nations, 187.
3. United Nations, 145.
4. United Nations, 12.
5. United Nations, 104.
6. Sue Monk Kidd and Ann Kidd Taylor, *Traveling with Pomegranates: A Mother-Daughter Story* (New York: Viking, 2009).

II. LISTEN TO YOUR MORAL COMPASS

Advice for Aspiring Preachers: David Nagler

1. Amos 7:14 (New International Version).
2. Matt. 5:45 (New Living Translation).
3. Martin Luther, *Lectures on Romans*, trans. and ed. Wilhelm Pauck (Louisville: Westminster John Knox Press, 2006), 208.

Healing Political Bodies and the Body Politic: Ched Myers

1. Prov. 22:22 (New Revised Standard Version).
2. Ps. 146:7–9 (NRSV).
3. James 2:1–4 (NRSV).
4. Mark 7:26 (NRSV).
5. This phrase is cited in *Pirke de-Rabbi Eliezer* 29, which is admittedly a very late source (an 8th century CE aggadic-midrashic work on the Torah).
6. Mark 7:27 (NRSV).
7. Mark 7:28 (NRSV).

8. Mark 7:29 (NRSV).
9. Mark 7:15 (NRSV).
10. Mark 7:27 (NRSV).
11. Mark 6:42, 8:8 (NRSV).

Living on This Planet so Others Can Live: Sallie McFague

1. Martin Luther, *Lectures on Romans*, trans. and ed. Wilhelm Pauck (Louisville: Westminster John Knox Press, 2006), 159.
2. "Distribution of the Global Population 2018, by Continent," Statista, accessed January 11, 2019, https://www.statista.com/statistics/237584 /distribution-of-the-world-population-by-continent/.
3. Irenaeus, "Irenaeus Against Heresies," in *The Ante-Nicene Fathers: Translations of the Writings of the Fathers down to A.D. 325*, American ed., eds. Alexander Roberts and James Donaldson, vol. 1, *The Apostolic Fathers with Justin Martyr and Irenaeus* (New York: Scribner, 1913), 490.
4. Augustine, "Chapter 6:41–59," tract. 26 in *A Select Library of the Nicene and Post-Nicene Fathers of the Christian Church*, ed. Philip Schaff, trans. John Gibb and James Innes, vol. 7, *St. Augustin: Homilies on the Gospel of John, Homilies on the First Epistle of John, Soliloquies* (New York: Christian Literature Company, 1888), 170.

A Letter to My Bishop: George S. Johnson

1. Douglas John Hall, *The Cross in Our Context: Jesus in a Suffering World* (Minneapolis: Fortress Press, 2003), 171.
2. Walter Brueggemann, *The Covenanted Self: Explorations in Law and Covenant*, ed. Patrick D. Miller (Minneapolis: Fortress Press, 1999), 35.
3. Jeorg Rieger, *God and the Excluded: Visions and Blind Spots in Contemporary Theology* (Minneapolis: Fortress Press, 2001), 162.
4. Dorothee Sölle, *On Earth as in Heaven: A Liberation Spirituality of Sharing*, trans. Marc Batko (Louisville: Westminster John Knox Press, 1993), 7.
5. Shane Claiborne, *The Irresistible Revolution: Living as an Ordinary Radical*, ReadHowYouWant ed. (Sydney: Accessible Publishing Systems, 2010), 5.
6. Claiborne, 86.

Sanctity of the Family: Paul Tellström

1. Rom. 13:1–7 (New Revised Standard Version).
2. Matt. 25:45 (NRSV).
3. Marcus J. Borg and John Dominic Crossan, *The First Paul: Reclaiming the Radical Visionary behind the Church's Conservative Icon* (New York: HarperCollins, 2009), 117–118, PDF.
4. Rom. 12:14 (NRSV).
5. Susan Henry-Crowe, "A Shocking Violation of the Spirit of the Gospel," Church and Society: The United Methodist Church, the United

Methodist Church, June 15, 2018, https://www.umcjustice.org/
news-and-stories/a-shocking-violation-of-the-spirit-of-the-gospel-697.
6. Rom. 13:10 (NRSV).
7. Isa. 10:1–2 (New International Version).

Why Justice Is Not Secondary: George S. Johnson

1. Shane Claiborne, *The Irresistible Revolution: Living as an Ordinary Radical*,
ReadHowYouWant ed. (Sydney: Accessible Publishing Systems, 2010), 86.
2. Hugh O'Shaughnessy, "Hélder Câmara—Brazil's Archbishop of the Poor,"
Guardian, October 13, 2009, https://www.theguardian.com
/commentisfree/belief/2009/oct/13/brazil-helder-camara.
3. Matt. 5:10 (New Revised Standard Version).
4. 1 John 4:7 (NRSV).

III. YOUR VOICE CAN MAKE A DIFFERENCE

1. Matt. 5:16 (New International Version).

What One Person Can Do: Lowell Erdahl

1. 1 Thess. 5:17 (New International Version).
2. "Barth in Retirement," *Time*, May 31, 1963, http://content.time
.com/time/subscriber/article/0,33009,896838,00.html.
3. Domenico Losurdo, *Non-Violence: A History beyond the Myth*, trans.
Gregory Elliott (Lanham, MD: Lexington Books, 2015), 156.
4. Isa. 2:4 (New Revised Standard Version).
5. Isa. 9:6 (NRSV).
6. Acts 3:15 (NRSV).

Coming Out Queer, Coming Out Christian: Brenda Bos

1. Queer is a term historically used to shame homosexuals. Today, many in
the LGBTQIA+ community use this word not only as an umbrella term
but also to identify oneself as not easily defined. I love this word for exactly
that reason. I also like the verb to queer, which means to analyze and
critique cultural norms and assumptions. To queer the Bible, for example,
is to read it through the lens of the LGBTQIA+ community and look
for hidden relationships and compassion in interactions either between
Biblical characters or with God. This does not necessarily mean the reader
assumes two characters were romantically involved; but it may mean the
two characters had a deeper connection than the surface reading indicates.
Great richness and diversity may be discovered in the Bible when one
queers it.
2. LGBTQIA+ is one of the currently accepted acronyms for the lesbian,
gay, bisexual, transgender, queer, intersex, and asexual community, with
the plus sign indicating that the number of gender and sexual expressions

and identities continues beyond these letters. As noted above, queer is occasionally used instead of this acronym, but queer continues to have mixed connotations, especially outside the LGBTQIA+ community. I acknowledge this acronym may be outdated within six months of this essay's publication.

3. Raymond A. Smith, ed., *Encyclopedia of AIDS: A Social, Political, Cultural, and Scientific Record of the HIV Epidemic* (New York City: Penguin Books, 2001), 642.

4. "Facts about Suicide," the Trevor Project (website), the Trevor Project, accessed October 7, 2018, https://www.thetrevorproject.org/resources /preventing-suicide/facts-about-suicide/.

5. Laura Kann et al., "Youth Risk Behavior Surveillance—United States, 2017," *MMWR Surveillance Summaries* 67, no. 8, (June 15, 2018): 26, https://www.cdc.gov/healthyyouth/data/yrbs/pdf/2017/ss6708.pdf.

6. Kann et al., 8.

7. Laura E. Durso and Gary J. Gates, *Serving Our Youth: Findings from a National Survey of Service Providers Working with Lesbian, Gay, Bisexual, and Transgender Youth Who Are Homeless or at Risk of Becoming Homeless* (Los Angeles. The Williams Institute with True Colors Fund and The Palette Fund, 2012), https://williamsinstitute.law.ucla.edu/wp content /uploads/Durso-Gates-LGBT-Homeless-Youth-Survey-July-2012.pdf.

8. Elizabeth M. Edman, *Queer Virtue: What LGBTQ People Know about Life and Love and How It Can Revitalize Christianity*, (Boston: Beacon Press, 2016).

Preaching Grace: Christine M. Smith

1. Susan Brooks Thistlethwaite and Mary Potter Engel, eds., *Lift Every Voice: Constructing Christian Theologies from the Underside* (San Francisco: Harper & Row, 1990), 165.

2. Thistlethwaite and Engel, 165.

3. John E. Fortunato, *Embracing the Exile: Healing Journeys of Gay Christians* (San Francisco: Harper & Row, 1982), 86.

4. M. Douglas Meeks, "Love and the Hope for a Just Society," in Frederic B. Burnham, Charles S. McCoy, and M. Douglas Meeks, eds., *Love: The Foundation of Hope in the Theology of Jürgen Moltmann and Elisabeth Moltmann-Wendel* (San Francisco: Harper & Row, 1988), 44–45. The image of home or household is a central one for Meeks's understanding of justice and God's economy.

5. Marsie Silvestro, "Blessing Song," in Diann Neu, ed., *Women Church Celebrations: Feminist Liturgies for the Lenten Season* (Silver Spring, MD: WATER/Resources, 1985), 52.

6. Chris Glaser, *Come Home! Reclaiming Spirituality and Community as Gay Men and Lesbians* (San Francisco: Harper & Row, 1990), 213.

Standing Your Ground: Paul Tellström

1. Bron Yocum, "A New Year's Prayer," *With Words If Necessary* (blog), December 31, 2016, https://bronyocum.org/2016/12/30/a-new-years-prayer/.
2. Rom. 8:31 (New International Version).

New Wineskins, New Dimensions: Larry Rasmussen

1. Luke 5:36–39 (New Revised Standard Version).
2. Nicole Krauss, *The History of Love* (New York: Norton, 2005), 8.
3. Jerome S. Bruner and Leo Postman, "On the Perception of Incongruity: A Paradigm," *Journal of Personality* 18, no. 2 (December 1949): 206–223, https://onlinelibrary.wiley.com/doi/abs/10.1111/j.1467-6494.1949 .tb01241.x.
4. Elizabeth Kolbert, *The Sixth Extinction: An Unnatural History* (New York: Henry Holt, 2014), 92–93.
5. Matt. 21:42 (NRSV).
6. Luke 24:21 (NRSV).
7. Howard Thurman, *The Living Wisdom of Howard Thurman: A Visionary for Our Time*, read by Howard Thurman et al. (Louisville, CO: Sounds True, 2010), audible audiobook, 7 hr., 37 min.
8. Heb. 11:1 (NRSV).
9. E. B. White, introduction to *Onward and Upward in the Garden*, by Katharine White, ed. E. B. White (Boston: Beacon Press, 1979), xviii–xix.

The Teachings of the Reverend Dr. James M. Lawson, Jr.: Ashley Herndon

1. Ralph McGill, *The Fleas Come with the Dog* (New York: Abingdon Press, 1954), 29.

Acknowledgments

I ACKNOWLEDGE WITH DEEP thanks our talented and efficient editor, Sharon Goldinger. She has remarkable ability and experience in managing books from their inception to completion. She kept me on track, offered astute suggestions, and corrected my misconceptions of how to birth a book. I respect her knowledge and professionalism.

Bil Aulenbach is a true friend in that he introduced me to Sharon Goldinger, our editor. He offered me words of encouragement and shared his knowledge as I embarked on and pursued this project.

Heartfelt thanks to the many authors who freely gave of their time and talent to write articles that encourage us to break the silence by listening, discerning, voting, writing, speaking, and organizing. The book truly was a group effort by a variety of knowledgeable people.

Thanks also to those who came to our home to read important articles to me since my eyesight is diminished. You had to use your outdoor voice due to my lack of hearing. Your willingness to leave what you were doing to help me fills me with appreciation.

Keith Boyum deserves sincere thanks for using his expertise in technology to research some information for me, as well as his assistance with marketing.

I would be remiss if I didn't thank our daughter Joy for her assistance in typing some of the articles. She lived up to her name as she joyfully attempted to read my snarly penmanship.

Thanks to all of you—you know who you are—who listened patiently when I went on and on about my favorite topic, the book. Your willingness to listen and to offer suggestions warmed my heart.

Index

Contributing Authors

Brenda Bos is a pastor in Southern California in the Evangelical Lutheran Church in America (ECLA). She is an advocate for LGBTQIA+, the homeless, and those who were told they do not have a place in the church.

Walter Brueggemann is William Marcellus McPheeters Professor Emeritus of Old Testament at Columbia Theological Seminary. He has written dozens of books, including *Journey to the Common Good* and *Interrupting Silence: God's Command to Speak Out.*

Herbert W. Chilstrom is bishop emeritus of the Evangelical Lutheran Church in America and the author of several books.

John B. Cobb Jr. taught theology at the Claremont School of Theology until his retirement in 1990. He continues to work with the Center for Process Studies at the Institute for the Postmodern Development of China, Pando Populus, and the Claremont Institute for Process Studies.

Lowell Erdahl was a pastor at Farmington Lutheran Church, Farmington, Minnesota; assistant professor at Luther Seminary, St. Paul; senior pastor at University Lutheran Church of Hope, Minneapolis; bishop of the Southeastern Minnesota District, ELC; and then bishop of St. Paul Area Synod of the ELCA. He is the author of ten books.

Wesley Granberg-Michaelson has written seven books on theology and formerly served as general secretary of the Reformed Church of America, director of Church and Society for the World Council of Churches, and associate editor of *Sojourners* magazine.

Ashley D. Herndon is a native Georgian blessed with two families who practice agape. He was educated at Mercer University and Georgia State University, receiving a degree in urban life. Blessed is the operative word, having met the author of this book since moving to Irvine, California, and Rev. Dr. Martin L. King, Jr. in both business and in his home.

Rev. Dr. Thomas K. Johnson was ordained ELCA pastor for thirty-six years and has been director of the Center for Lutheran Studies at Claremont School of Theology and professor for twenty-three years. He has published five works, most recently *Celebrating the Seasons of Baptismal Living* with Augsburg Fortress. He lives in Claremont, California, with his wife, Julie.

Vivian Elaine Johnson, MA, is an author of several articles dealing with creative coping from life's losses and a co-creator of LifeStories, an intergenerational communication game.

Sallie McFague taught theology for many years at the Vanderbilt University Divinity School in Nashville, Tennessee, and is presently Scholar in Residence at the Vancouver School of Theology in Vancouver, British Columbia, Canada. Her interest in religious language and its relationship to climate change has resulted in many books, chief among them being *A New Climate for Theology: God, the World, and Global Warming* and *Blessed Are the Consumers: Climate Change and the Practice of Restraint*, both published by Fortress Press.

Ched Myers is an activist theologian working in the Ventura River Watershed of southern California with Bartimaeus Cooperative Ministries (www.bcm-net.org). His many publications can be found at www.ChedMyers.org.

David Nagler is a surfer and a theologian, in that order. He has served congregations in California and Oregon. He has also directed interfaith dialogue in Madagascar and was the CEO and pastor of Central City Lutheran Mission in San Bernardino, California.

Larry Rasmussen is Reinhold Niebuhr Professor Emeritus of Social Ethics, Union Theological Seminary, New York City. He and his wife, Nyla, live in Santa Fe, New Mexico.

Richard Rohr is a Franciscan friar based in Albuquerque, New Mexico. He is the author of thirty-two books on spirituality and religion, the most recent being *The Universal Christ: How a Forgotten Reality Can Change Everything We See, Hope For, and Believe.*

Dan Roschke is a pastor in the Evangelical Lutheran Church in America. He has served congregations in Missouri, Southern California, and northern Virginia, where he currently resides with his spouse and their two children.

Christine M. Smith is an associate professor of preaching and worshipping at United Theological Seminary of Twin Cities, New Brighton, Minnesota. She is the author of three books, including *Preaching as Weeping, Confession, and Resistance.*

Rev. Paul Tellström has been the senior pastor at the Irvine United Congregational Church, UCC, for thirteen years. His work with that church is explored in a chapter of Paul Nixon's book *We Refused to Lead a Dying Church!: Churches That Came Back Against All Odds.*

Jim Wallis is the editor-in-chief of *Sojourners* magazine and author of twelve books, including his most recent book, *America's Original Sin: Racism, White Privilege, and the Bridge to a New America.* He also served on President Obama's White House Advisory Council on Faith-Based and Neighborhood Partnerships.

About the Author

GEORGE S. JOHNSON is a retired Lutheran pastor who lives with his wife, Vivian, in Irvine, California. After attending Augustana College, the Lutheran Bible Institute, and Luther Seminary, he was ordained in 1962. He later earned a master of theology from Luther Seminary in St. Paul, Minnesota, where his thesis was on the theology of P. T. Forsyth, a Scottish theologian. He received his doctor of ministry degree from Claremont School of Theology in California. George served parishes in California and Minnesota for more than thirty years.

The Johnsons took their daughters, Sonja and Joy, with them to Sweden for a year in 1979, where George did independent study at the Dag Hammarskjöld Institute. George also traveled to other Scandinavian countries to study hunger and justice issues. When they returned to the States, George became the director of the Hunger Program for the former American Lutheran Church (1980–1987). He lectured on development education and liberation theology in South Africa and India.

George served as advisor to the Committee on Economic Justice at the 1984 Assembly of the Lutheran World Federation in Budapest, Hungary. He also accompanied C. Dean Freudenberger to Africa to study food, farming, and hunger issues. After retirement, he served as an interim pastor and became the director of Third World Opportunities, where he took groups to Mexico for consciousness raising and service. Reading, writing, preaching, lecturing, and travel have kept him connected and current on poverty, hunger, justice, and oppression issues.

George has written and published educational material for church groups and classes. At San Marcos Lutheran he taught "Practicing the Faith," and at Irvine Congregational Church he taught "Gandhi, Bonhoeffer, and King," as well as "Good News to the Poor."

George received distinguished alumni awards from Augustana Academy and Claremont School of Theology. He is an ardent fan of the San Francisco Giants baseball team and an equally ardent fan of maple nut ice cream.

His published works include the following:

Courage to Think Differently (Bang Printing, 2013)

Beyond Guilt: Christian Response to Suffering, five printings (rev. ed., 2000)

How to Start Small Groups and Keep Them Going (Augsburg Fortress, 1995)

Following Jesus: Encouragement from the Beatitudes for a Troubled World (Augsburg Fortress, 1995)

Critical Decisions in Following Jesus: Sermons for Sundays after Pentecost (CSS, 1992)

Evangelism and the Poor: A Biblical Challenge for the Church, with Ana DeGarcia (Augsburg Fortress, 1986)

You can reach George at vivianelaine0@gmail.com.